THE DEHYDRATOR COOKBOOK
Revised Edition

Joanna White

BRISTOL PUBLISHING ENTERPRISES, INC.
San Leandro, California

a nitty gritty® cookbook

Printed in the United States of America.

ISBN 1-55867-195-1

Cover design: Frank J. Paredes
Cover photography: John A. Benson
Food stylist: Susan Massey
Illustrator: James Balkovek

CONTENTS

DEHYDRATING FOODS: GENERAL INFORMATION

Welcome to the wonderful food-preserving method of dehydrating! In the pages that follow, you will learn the advantages of this easy, economical approach to preserving fruits, vegetables, meats, poultry and fish, and all of the techniques required. You will be introduced to some delicious recipes as well.

This book is divided into four sections: general information about dehydrating, including drying techniques; dehydrating fruits and vegetables; dehydrating meats, poultry and fish; and a section on other ways to utilize the dehydrator. The fruits and vegetables are organized alphabetically. Recipes follow each fruit or vegetable to give you examples of ways to use the preserved foods. Since most recipes call for rehydrated produce, you can even use fresh produce to make these recipes.

In each section, up to five categories related to dehydrating foods are discussed: preparing foods for dehydrating; pretreating foods before dehydrating; storing dehydrated foods; rehydrating dehydrated foods; and cooking with dehydrated foods.

This book is different from other dehydrating books, as it uses lower dehydrating temperatures and natural pretreatment techniques in order to retain as many nutrients and digestive enzymes in the foods as possible. However, it is important to read the manufacturer's instructions and be familiar with your specific make and model of dehydrator before beginning.

ADVANTAGES OF DEHYDRATING FOODS

- Dehydrating is inexpensive and is the least time-consuming of all food preserving methods. Dehydrating is superior to canning, as the high temperatures needed to process canned foods can destroy as much as 65% of the original food value, especially vitamin C, thiamin and riboflavin.
- Dehydrated foods take up little storage space, keep well without refrigeration and are low in bulk and weight. Since dried foods reduce to about 1/4 the original weight, they are concentrated nutritional powerhouses.
- Dehydrating is easy to do and the results are nutritious and versatile. Dehydrated food is about equal to frozen food in nutritional value.
- Dehydrating is a great way to use excessive produce during peak seasons.
- Dehydrating is an effective way to preserve leftovers. For example, stews, sauces, bean dishes and other prepared foods can be dried to use at a later date.
- Dehydrated foods are excellent for backpacking, camping, fishing, skiing or any outdoor sport.
- The dehydrator can be used to make homemade fruit leathers, one of the most popular foods for kids. Leathers make delicious all-natural, candy-like snacks.

USING AN ELECTRIC FOOD DEHYDRATOR

There are many methods for dehydrating foods, such as sun-drying and stovetop-drying, but using an electric food dehydrator is the safest and most efficient way. **It is extremely important that you become familiar with the manufacturer's instructions for your dehydrator before beginning**. While experimenting with different foods, drying times and temperatures is encouraged, it is a good idea to start with the recommendations of the manufacturer and this book before trying new things.

DEHYDRATOR FEATURES

The features of a dehydrator differ with the manufacturer and model number. Some dehydrators have a temperature control gauge, while some do not. If your model has no temperature control, place a thermometer inside the dehydrator to obtain an accurate reading. You may have to adjust the drying time or thickness of the food that you are drying based on the temperature of the dehydrator.

Many accessories are available for dehydrators. Standard drying trays have numerous holes through which air circulates to dehydrate the food. Solid drying trays have no holes, and feature rims to hold liquids while drying. A solid tray can be simulated by covering a regular tray with plastic wrap before adding the food. Other accessories include netted sheets for drying small foods, jerky presses for pressing meats and poultry, nonstick sheets for removing dried foods, and yogurt-making containers.

DEHYDRATING TERMINOLOGY

Depending on the type of food used, the results of dehydration will vary.

CRISP: The food breaks easily when bent. Test foods for crispness when they have fully cooled; warm dried foods may not be crisp even when fully dried. Dehydrate apples, bananas, green beans, cabbage, celery, citrus fruits, corn, garlic, leeks, mushrooms, potatoes, radishes, rhubarb, tomatoes, croutons and cooked meats until crisp.

BRITTLE: The food crumbles easily into smaller pieces. Test foods for brittleness when fully cooled. Dehydrate artichokes, asparagus, avocados, beets, berries, broccoli, Brussels sprouts, carrots, ginger, onions, parsnips, peas, peppers, zucchini, prepared foods, herbs and nuts until brittle.

LEATHERY: The food is shriveled and bendable, but will not crack or crumble. Dehydrate blueberries, cherries, cranberries, dates, eggplant, grapes, pineapple, plums and strawberries until leathery.

PLIABLE: The food is soft and easy to fold; it will not break when bent. Dehydrate apricots, cantaloupe, kiwi fruit, mangoes, nectarines, papayas, peaches, pears, watermelon, and meat, poultry or fish jerky until pliable.

PREPARING FOODS FOR DEHYDRATING

1. Use only the highest quality foods for dehydrating. Blemished or bruised fruit will not keep well and may spoil the whole batch. Fruit should be fully ripe so that the sugar content is at its peak. If dehydrating meats, fish or poultry, use very fresh and lean products.

2. Wash all produce well to remove dirt, insect larvae and bacteria. Trim away any bruised or soft spots. Remove any visible fat from meats or poultry.

3. Remove pits, stems and peelings, if desired, of fruits or vegetables. Produce peelings contain many vitamins, but increase the drying time, which in turn causes vitamin loss and sometimes a slightly bitter taste. Any waxed peelings should definitely be removed before drying. Remove bones, if any, from meat, poultry or fish you intend to dehydrate.

4. Cut fruits or vegetables to a consistent size so that they will dry at the same rate. A food processor's slicing blade works well because it cuts uniformly and works quickly, preserving nutrients. Keep pieces small, as larger pieces take longer to dry and nutrients will be lost. Meats or poultry can be sliced very thinly against the grain, or ground (see pages 146-51 for specific information).

PRETREATING DEHYDRATED FOODS

This book uses 9 natural methods for pretreating foods. There are other options, such as sodium bisulfite and sulfur, but I do not recommend them here.

Ascorbic Acid: This is used for fruits that tend to turn brown when exposed to air. Otherwise known as powdered vitamin C, use 3 tablespoons ascorbic acid powder per quart of water to make an ascorbic acid solution. Slice the fruit directly into the solution, let stand for 2 minutes, drain well and place on trays to dry.

Citric Acid: Also used to prevent browning of fruits, citric acid can add a fresh flavor to the dried product. This book uses lemon juice (you can also use pineapple juice) to create a citric acid bath. Slice the fruit directly into lemon juice and let stand in the undiluted juice for about 2 minutes. Drain fruit well and place on trays to dry.

Steam-Blanching: This is ideal for most vegetables, since it keeps their internal temperature low, thus retaining more vitamins and enzymes. It also helps retain more of the vegetable's natural color. Place vegetables in a steamer basket in a saucepan. Add water to the saucepan, being careful not to let the water touch the food. Cover with a lid and steam for the recommended time. Immediately chill the vegetables under cold running water, drain thoroughly and place on trays to dry.

Water-Blanching: This method is quicker than steam-blanching, but more nutrients will be leached out in the water. Place the prepared produce in boiling water and measure the time from when the water resumes boiling. Boil for the recommended time, chill under cold running water, drain thoroughly and place on trays to dry.

Syrup-Blanching: Use this to retain color and add flavor to dried fruits that are intended for rehydrating. Combine 1 cup sugar, 1 cup corn syrup, 2 cups water and 1 tsp. ascorbic acid powder in a heavy saucepan. Bring ingredients to a boil and add prepared fruit. Reduce heat to low and simmer for 5 to 10 minutes, depending on the variety and thickness of the fruit. Syrup-blanched fruit takes longer to dehydrate.

Checking: This is used for fruits that have a natural protective coating, such as grapes, blueberries, cherries, cranberries and plums, to make their skins more porous and allow moisture to escape. Checking helps the fruit dry considerably faster, which reduces nutrient loss. Drop fruits into boiling water until the skins burst slightly, about 2 minutes. Drain fruit well and place on trays to dry.

Cooking: Some vegetables, such as beets, should be completely cooked before being dehydrated. It is also possible to dehydrate cooked prepared foods, such as roasted meats and poultry, soups, stews, sauces and even cooked canned foods.

Marinating: Marinating is used when drying meats and poultry. It adds flavor to the final product, and the salt in the marinade helps to preserve the food.

Brining and Curing: This method is used when making fish jerky. The fish is first soaked in a salt-brine solution (1 cup salt to 2 quarts cold water) and is then rubbed with a cure mixture and marinated for a period of time. The salt in both the brine and the cure helps to draw the moisture from the fish and acts as a "cooking" agent. The curing step adds flavor to the final product.

STORING DEHYDRATED FOODS

1. Check food for dryness. Different-sized pieces will dry at different rates. Remove only the pieces that are dry from the dehydrator and leave the others for a longer period. To be sure the food is dry, tear a piece in half and check for moisture.

2. Once you are sure the food is completely dry, store the dried foods in glass jars, plastic containers or food-grade heavy plastic freezer bags inserted into metal or plastic containers with tight-fitting lids. Fill each container as full as possible in order to eliminate air.

3. Label each package of dried food with the contents, date and, if desired, the rehydrating procedure. You may also wish to list the volume measurement and/or weight of the food before dehydrating, which will be useful when using the rehydrated foods in recipes.

4. Store the packaged dried food in a dry, dark, cool area. The lower the temperature, the longer the shelf life will be. Light exposure will shorten shelf life. Ideally, dried foods should be kept below 60°. Dried meat, poultry, fish and nuts can be stored in the freezer for extra protection.

5. If the food has been dried properly, it should last from 6 months to 1 year. If it is stored at low temperatures, the shelf life can even be longer. Rotate your dried food to ensure quality and nutritional value.

7. Periodically check your stored foods for mold, moisture or insects. If there is mold or insects, discard the food.

REHYDRATING DRIED FOODS

Dehydrated meats are usually eaten in their dried state as snacks, but they can be rehydrated and used in casseroles, soups or stews. See page 152 for more information on rehydrating dried meats. There are 3 general methods for rehydrating produce. Follow the instructions under each fruit or vegetable for specific information.

1. Steam dried fruits or vegetables until plumped.

2. Cover the dried produce with cold water or fruit juice and let stand until plumped; drain.

3. Cover the dried produce with boiling water or fruit juice and let stand until plumped; drain.

GENERAL GUIDELINES FOR REHYDRATING PRODUCE

- Some dried fruits and vegetables can be used directly in recipes, such as baked items, without rehydrating. Dried vegetables can be used directly in heated liquids like soups, stews or sauces, but the vegetables may be tough.

- Vegetables are better if they are allowed to soak long enough to reabsorb most of their water before using for cooking.

- Vegetables rehydrate slower than fruits because they have lost more water.

- Rehydrating times vary according to the type of fruit or vegetable. It is important not to leave the produce in the soaking water for more than 2 hours without refrigeration due to the danger of bacterial growth.

- Use just enough liquid to cover the vegetables and fruits. The quantity of liquid may vary depending on the type of produce used, but the standard measure is: for every 1 cup dried vegetables or fruits, use $1\frac{1}{2}$ cups liquid to rehydrate.

- Do not add salt or sugar when rehydrating vegetables or fruits because it inhibits water absorption.

COOKING WITH DEHYDRATED FOODS

VEGETABLES

- For the best nutrition, with the exception of greens, rehydrate vegetables in cold water just to cover. Let stand until close to the original texture before cooking according to the directions in the recipe. Greens should be just covered with boiling water and simmered until tender.

- When substituting dried vegetables for fresh vegetables in recipes, 1 cup dried vegetables equals about 3 cups fresh.

- Dried vegetables can be added to hot dishes without rehydrating. Use 1 cup additional water in your recipe for every 1 cup dried vegetables in stews. Use 2 cups additional water for every 1 cup dried vegetables in soups.
- For extra nutrition, cook vegetables in the liquid that was used to rehydrate them.

FRUITS

- If the dried fruit is to be used in a cooked dish, pour boiling water over the fruit, cover and let stand for up to 2 hours, until tender.
- Use the fruit-soaking liquid in recipes to add the residual nutrients.

MEATS, POULTRY AND FISH

- Reconstitute dried meats and poultry and use in hot entrées or appetizer dips.
- Dehydrated fish is not recommended for cooking, as it contains a great deal of salt. It is best used as a snack food.

In this book, follow the instructions that precede each food type and use the foods in the delicious recipes that follow.

APPLES

PREPARATION: Wash, peel if desired, core and cut into ¼-inch slices or chop. Peels contain a lot of nutrients, but have a tendency to make fruit tougher and take longer to dehydrate.

PRETREATMENT: Ascorbic acid. Soak in solution for 2 to 3 minutes; drain.

DEHYDRATE: Dry sliced apples at 100° for about 6 to 8 hours, until slightly crisp; dry chopped apples for 5 to 6 hours.

REHYDRATE: Soak in hot water for about 10 to 15 minutes; drain.

LEATHER: Excellent for leather (see pages 141-45). If desired, add about ¼ tsp. cinnamon, nutmeg, allspice, ginger or cloves to each quart of apple puree. Naturally sweet apple puree can be mixed with more tart fruit purees.

NOTE
- If you have apple trees, consider purchasing an automatic apple peeler, which peels, cores and slices apples in seconds.

APPLE PIE

When apples are in season, consider dehydrating them, especially the varieties that are good for baking, such as Golden Delicious and pippin.

4½ cups boiling water
4 cups dried apples
one 9-inch double pastry crust, unbaked
½-1 cup sugar
1 tsp. cinnamon
1 tbs. dried lemon peel
2 tbs. tapioca
1 tbs. butter

Heat oven to 375°. Pour boiling water over apples and let stand for about 30 minutes; drain and reserve liquid. Line a 9-inch pie pan with ½ of the pastry crust. In a saucepan, combine apple liquid, sugar, cinnamon and lemon peel and heat to boiling. Add tapioca and boil for 1 minute. Remove mixture from heat and add butter, stirring until butter melts. Stir in rehydrated apples, cool mixture and pour into pastry-lined pie pan. Cover with remaining pastry, fold bottom pastry edges over top pastry edges and crimp with a fork. With a knife, cut about 5 vents in top crust. Bake for about 40 minutes or until crust is golden brown.

APPLE WALNUT CAKE

Cakes are a great way to use dehydrated fruits because the appearance of dehydrated fruit is not important. Sour cream makes this cake wonderfully moist.

3 cups all-purpose flour
1 cup sugar
4 tsp. baking powder
1 tsp. salt
1 tsp. cinnamon
1 cup milk

½ cup butter, softened
4 eggs
2 cups rehydrated dried apples
1 cup sour cream
1 cup chopped toasted walnuts
½ cup sugar

Heat oven to 375°. In a bowl, mix together flour, 1 cup sugar, baking powder, salt and cinnamon. In another bowl, mix milk, butter and 2 of the eggs until blended. Add dry ingredients and blend until smooth. Stir in rehydrated apples and pour into a greased 9-x-13-inch baking pan. Blend sour cream with remaining 2 eggs and spread over batter. Mix walnuts and sugar together and sprinkle over batter. Bake for 35 to 45 minutes, or until a knife inserted into the center comes out clean. Cool and cut into squares.

SOUR CREAM APPLE SQUARES

Makes 32

This wonderful, moist dessert can be cut into small squares and served as cookies, or cut into large squares and served with ice cream as a dessert.

2 cups all-purpose flour
2 cups brown sugar, packed
1/2 cup butter, softened
2 cups chopped rehydrated apples
1 cup chopped nuts
1 cup sour cream
1 egg
1 tsp. vanilla extract
2 tsp. cinnamon
1 tsp. baking soda
1/2 tsp. salt

Heat oven to 350°. With a mixer, combine flour, brown sugar and butter and press 2¾ cups of the mixture into a greased 9-x-13-inch pan. In a bowl, mix apples, nuts, sour cream, egg, vanilla, cinnamon, soda and salt until blended and pour over crust. Crumble remaining brown sugar mixture over the top. Bake for 25 to 35 minutes, until a knife inserted into the center comes out clean. Cool and cut into squares.

APPLE-SAUSAGE SAUTÉ

This quick, simple dish for breakfast or brunch comes from the maple syrup state, Vermont. To make it traditional, serve with baked beans and brown bread or baking-powder biscuits.

1 lb. pork sausage links or patties
1 cup pure maple syrup
½ cup white or cider vinegar
3 cups rehydrated apple rings

Heat oven to 200°. In a skillet, sauté sausage over medium-high heat until golden brown. Drain on paper towels, place on a baking sheet and keep warm in oven. Mix maple syrup with vinegar in a saucepan and heat over medium heat until bubbling. Reduce heat to low, add rehydrated apple rings and simmer uncovered until apples are tender-crisp, about 5 minutes. Arrange apple rings on a platter with sausage, pour syrup mixture over the top and serve immediately.

APRICOTS

PREPARATION: Wash, halve and remove pits.

PRETREATMENT: Optional. There is no noticeable difference when treated with ascorbic acid. However, for better color and flavor if planning to rehydrate, syrup-blanch apricots.

DEHYDRATE: Place apricots cut-side down on trays. Dry at 100° for about 48 hours for untreated apricots and 60 hours for syrup-blanched apricots, until pliable with no pockets of moisture.

REHYDRATE: For cooking, soak in hot water for 15 minutes. For baking, apricots can be used dried.

LEATHER: Excellent for leather (see pages 141-45).

NOTE
- Snipping with scissors is the best method for cutting dried apricots.
- Label the storage container with the original weight of the apricots for ease in using for recipes.

APRICOT SAUCE

This is a great sauce to serve over waffles, pancakes or even over desserts like bread pudding.

1 cup rehydrated apricots,
   liquid reserved
½ cup pure maple syrup
2 tbs. cornstarch
1 cup apricot nectar
1 tbs. lemon juice
3 tbs. honey
pinch cinnamon

Cut rehydrated apricots into slivers or small cubes and set aside. In a heavy saucepan, blend reserved apricot liquid with maple syrup, cornstarch, apricot nectar, lemon juice, honey and cinnamon. Cook, stirring, over medium heat until mixture thickens and bubbles. Stir in sliced apricots, heat through and serve.

APRICOT ZUCCHINI BREAD

Makes 2 loaves

This great recipe utilizes both dehydrated apricots and zucchini. Try rehydrating some extra apricots and mixing with cream cheese and a little confectioners' sugar to serve as a spread on this bread.

1 cup vegetable oil
2 cups sugar
1 tbs. vanilla extract
3 eggs
2 cups rehydrated grated zucchini, well drained
1 lb. rehydrated dried apricots, well drained, finely chopped

3 cups all-purpose flour
2 tsp. baking soda
1 tsp. baking powder
1 tsp. salt
2 tsp. nutmeg
1 cup chopped walnuts

Heat oven to 350°. Line 2 loaf pans with greased brown paper and grease sides of pans. In a bowl, beat oil, sugar and vanilla until blended. Add eggs one at a time, beating well between additions. Add zucchini and apricots and beat well. Sift flour, baking soda, baking powder, salt and nutmeg together and stir into egg mixture. Mix in nuts until incorporated. Pour batter into prepared pans and bake for about 50 minutes, or until a knife inserted into the center comes out clean. Cool for 10 minutes before removing bread from pans.

ARTICHOKES

PREPARATION: Wash, remove leaves, remove and discard the fuzzy chokes and cut the hearts into quarters.

PRETREATMENT: Steam-blanch for about 4 minutes; drain.

DEHYDRATE: Dry at 100° for about 18 hours, until brittle.

REHYDRATE: Soak in boiling water for about 15 minutes, adding a little lemon juice to help retain the color; drain well.

NOTES
- Canned artichokes dry beautifully.
- Dried artichoke hearts are good marinated or in appetizer dips.
- Artichokes are good for you, so don't neglect them in your diet.

MARINATED ARTICHOKE HEARTS

Makes 6 cups

Many recipes call for marinated artichoke hearts. Here's a way to make your own to use in antipasto platters, appetizers, salads, casseroles and even on pizza.

2 cups dried artichoke hearts
6 cups boiling water
lemon juice
½ cup white wine vinegar
½ cup water
2 cloves garlic, minced
½ tsp. sugar

½ tsp. dried thyme
1 tbs. salt
1 tsp. dried basil
1 tsp. dried oregano
¼ tsp. red pepper flakes
½ cup olive oil
½ cup vegetable oil

Drop dried artichoke hearts into boiling water with a little lemon juice and let stand for about 15 minutes, until artichokes are tender. Drain, pat dry and place in a clean jar. In a saucepan, bring white wine vinegar, water, garlic, sugar and seasonings to a boil. Pour mixture over artichokes in jar and add oils. Seal tightly and refrigerate for 1 week before using. Turn jar upside down occasionally to blend flavors. Keep refrigerated and use within 3 weeks.

ARTICHOKE PARMESAN DIP

This is a quick, simple and rich recipe that people are crazy about. Serve with French bread rounds, crackers or buttered and toasted pita bread wedges.

1 cup *Marinated Artichoke Hearts*, page 22, cut into small pieces
1 cup grated Parmesan cheese
1 cup mayonnaise
½ cup diced green chiles
chopped red bell pepper or diced green chiles for garnish

Heat oven to 350°. Drain artichokes. Mix artichoke hearts with cheese, mayonnaise and green chiles. Pour into a small ovenproof dish and bake for 20 minutes. Serve hot garnished with red pepper.

ASPARAGUS

PREPARATION: Wash and remove tough ends.

PRETREATMENT: Steam-blanch for about 3 minutes; drain.

DEHYDRATE: Dry at 100° for about 35 to 40 hours, depending on the size of stalks, until very dry and brittle.

REHYDRATE: Soak in hot water for about 30 minutes; drain. Stalks tend to remain slightly tough.

NOTE

- Asparagus has a very high water content, so it requires a long drying time. Make sure asparagus is very dry and brittle before storing to avoid mold.
- Dried asparagus is best used in recipes that require mashed asparagus. Or, cut it into pieces and mix it into a casserole dish.

PATÉ WITH ASPARAGUS

Makes 1 loaf

Dried asparagus creates an appealing look in this paté. The mayonnaise is also great in sandwiches or for dipping artichokes.

1 cup rehydrated spinach, drained
1 lb. ground pork
1 lb. lean ground beef
1 cup fresh breadcrumbs
1 tsp. dried sage
1 tsp. dried thyme
2 tsp. salt

1 tsp. pepper
1 tsp. dried rosemary
1 tbs. chopped fresh parsley
2 cloves garlic, minced
1 cup rehydrated asparagus spears
Asparagus Mayonnaise, follows

Heat oven to 350°. Mix spinach with remaining ingredients, except asparagus and mayonnaise. Press mixture into a ceramic loaf pan, layering rehydrated asparagus spears randomly throughout mixture. Bake for about 45 minutes, or until a thermometer registers 170° when inserted into the center; cool. Cover, place a brick or other weight on top of paté and chill overnight. To serve, invert paté onto a serving dish. Serve each portion with a dollop of *Asparagus Mayonnaise*.

Makes 2½ cups

ASPARAGUS MAYONNAISE

Mix together 2 cups mayonnaise, ½ cup mashed rehydrated asparagus, and balsamic vinegar, salt and pepper to taste.

AVOCADOS

PREPARATION: Peel, remove pit and cut into 1/4-inch slices.

PRETREATMENT: Ascorbic acid. Soak in solution for about 5 minutes; drain.

DEHYDRATE: Dry at 100° for about 60 hours, until brittle.

REHYDRATE: Soak in hot water for about 15 minutes; drain.

NOTE
- Because of their high oil content, avocados take a long time to dehydrate.
- Even with the ascorbic acid bath, avocados will turn a little brown.
- Use dehydrated avocados in recipes that call for mashed avocados, such as baked goods.

AVOCADO PECAN BREAD

Makes 2 loaves

This great, moist bread is easy to make and not affected by the slightly altered color of a rehydrated avocado.

2 eggs
1 cup mashed rehydrated avocado
1 cup buttermilk
2/3 cup vegetable oil
4 cups all-purpose flour

1 1/2 cups sugar
1 tsp. baking soda
1 tsp. baking powder
1/2 tsp. salt
1 1/2 cups chopped toasted pecans

Heat oven to 350°. Line 2 loaf pans with greased brown paper and grease sides of pans. With a mixer or food processor, mix eggs, avocado, buttermilk and oil until well blended. Add flour, sugar, baking soda, baking powder, salt and pecans. Mix just until blended; do not overmix. Pour batter into prepared pans. Bake for 1 hour, or until a knife inserted into the center comes out clean. Cool for 10 minutes before removing from pans.

AVOCADO MAYONNAISE

Can you imagine all the things you can do with avocado mayonnaise? Serve with your favorite sandwich combinations, on patés, on salads or in appetizer dips. The dehydrated avocado gives this mayonnaise a pale green color, which can be enhanced with a drop of green food coloring, if desired.

¼ cup rehydrated diced onion
½ cup mashed rehydrated avocado
1½ cups mayonnaise
2 tsp. Dijon mustard
1 tsp. lemon juice

1 tsp. balsamic or red wine vinegar
1 tsp. salt
pepper to taste
3 tbs. fresh grapefruit juice

With a food processor or blender, process onion and avocado until pureed. Add mayonnaise, mustard, lemon juice, vinegar, salt and pepper. Process for 15 seconds, until thick. Add grapefruit juice and process to mix. Taste and adjust seasonings.

BANANAS

PREPARATION: Peel and cut into ¼-inch slices. Avoid overripe bananas.

PRETREATMENT: Ascorbic acid. Soak in solution for 2 to 3 minutes; drain.

DEHYDRATE: Dry at 100° for about 55 hours, until crisp.

REHYDRATE: Soak in hot water for about 10 minutes; drain. About 1 cup tightly packed dried bananas will rehydrate to 2 cups.

LEATHER: Excellent for leather (see pages 141-45). Can be a little too sweet. Add a little ascorbic acid to prevent discoloration. Add bananas to less sweet fruit purees to achieve a nice flavor balance.

NOTE
- Dried bananas are great as a snack or used in trail mixes or cereals.
- Rehydrated bananas are good for baked products like breads, cakes and cookies.

BEST BANANA BREAD

Makes 2 loaves

This is my favorite banana bread recipe — what else can I say? Add about ½ cup chopped toasted walnuts if desired.

2 cups sugar
1 cup butter, softened
3 cups mashed rehydrated bananas
4 eggs
1 tsp. banana extract
2½ cups cake flour
2 tsp. baking soda
1 tsp. salt

Heat oven to 350°. Line 2 loaf pans with greased brown paper and grease sides of pans. With a mixer, blend sugar and butter until light and fluffy. Add bananas to butter mixture along with eggs and banana extract; beat well. Sift cake flour, soda and salt together and blend with banana mixture; do not overmix. Pour into prepared pans and bake for about 30 minutes, or until a knife inserted into the center comes out clean. Cool for 10 minutes before removing from pans.

BEANS, GREEN

PREPARATION: Wash, snip ends and cut into 1-inch pieces.

PRETREATMENT: Steam-blanch for about 4 minutes; drain. To tenderize beans before drying, place in a single layer on a baking sheet and freeze until solid, about 40 minutes.

DEHYDRATE: Dry at 100° for about 30 hours, until crisp.

REHYDRATE: Soak in cold water for at least 2 hours; or, soak in hot water for at least 1 hour; drain. You can add dried green beans directly to soups and stews. However, you may need to add additional liquid to the recipe.

NOTE
- Dried green beans are best served in hot main dishes like stews, soups or casseroles.

VEGETABLE BARLEY SOUP

Servings: 8

Endless combinations of vegetables can be used for this versatile soup. Be inventive with the seasoning and you'll never tire of this recipe. Serve with hearty bread and a fruit cobbler for dessert.

2 cups boiling water or vegetable stock
2 cups mixed dried green beans and
   other vegetables
½ cup dried diced onion
½ cup dried celery
3 cups vegetable stock
1 can (16 oz.) crushed tomatoes
¾ cup barley or wheat berries

salt and pepper to taste
1 clove garlic, minced
1 tsp. dried basil
½ tsp. dried thyme
1 tbs. dried parsley
3-4 tbs. butter
salt and pepper to taste

Pour 1½ cups of the boiling water over 2 cups mixed dried vegetables and let stand for at least 30 minutes. Pour ½ cup of the boiling water over onion and celery and let stand for 30 minutes; drain. Place 3 cups stock, tomatoes and barley in a large saucepan. Add seasonings, bring to a boil, reduce heat to low and simmer for 30 minutes. Melt butter in a skillet and sauté rehydrated onion and celery over medium heat until wilted. Add to saucepan with rehydrated mixed vegetables and simmer for about 20 minutes. Taste and adjust seasonings.

BEETS

PREPARATION: Wash and remove tops. Cut in half if large.

PRETREATMENT: Cooking. Steam beets until tender, about 20 to 30 minutes. Peel and cut into $\frac{1}{2}$-inch slices or shred.

DEHYDRATE: Dry sliced beets at 100° for about 12 to 15 hours, until brittle; dry shredded beets for 10 to 12 hours.

REHYDRATE: Soak in cold water for about 1 hour; drain. Or, soak overnight in the refrigerator; drain.

NOTE
- Dried beets can be finely ground and used to color and flavor sauces or salad dressings.
- To make recipe preparation a breeze, weigh the beets before dehydrating and label the package clearly with their original weight.

CHOCOLATE BEET CAKE

The secret ingredient in this delicious cake is beets. Their flavor is unnoticeable, but they add moisture and vitamins to the cake. Just don't tell anyone they are eating beets! An easy way to melt chocolate is to chop it into small pieces, place it in a bowl and cook it in the microwave on MEDIUM for about 1 minute; stir until smooth.

¾ cup rehydrated beets, liquid reserved
½ cup butter, softened
2¾ cups brown sugar, packed
3 eggs
2 tsp. vanilla extract
½ cup buttermilk
3 oz. unsweetened chocolate, melted
2 cups all-purpose flour
2 tsp. baking soda
½ tsp. salt
Chocolate Frosting, follows

Heat oven to 350°. Butter and flour two 9-inch cake pans. Finely chop rehydrated beets and mix with ¼ cup of the reserved beet liquid. With a mixer, beat butter and brown sugar until light and creamy. Add eggs, vanilla and buttermilk and beat until mixture is well blended. Add melted chocolate and beets and beat until well mixed. Add flour, baking soda and salt and beat well. If batter appears thick, add a small amount of beet liquid. Pour batter into prepared pans. Bake for 30 minutes or until cake just barely springs back to the touch. Cool and frost layers with *Chocolate Frosting*. Assemble layers and let stand until frosting is set, about 30 minutes.

CHOCOLATE FROSTING

Makes about 2 cups

2 cups heavy cream
16 oz. semisweet chocolate chips
2 tsp. vanilla extract

In a heavy saucepan, heat cream until just below the boiling point. Remove pan from heat and stir in chocolate chips until melted. Stir in vanilla. Refrigerate mixture, stirring every 10 minutes until mixture thickens to the texture of pudding; then, stir every 5 minutes until mixture thickens to the texture of fudge, about 1 hour or more.

RUSSIAN VEGETABLE SOUP (BORSCHT)

Servings: 12

This traditional soup utilizes many rehydrated vegetables.

2 tbs. oil
2 tbs. butter
1 cup rehydrated diced onions
1 tsp. minced garlic
3/4 lb. rehydrated shredded beets
1 cup rehydrated celery
2/3 cup chopped fresh parsley
1 cup rehydrated grated parsnips
2 tsp. sugar
1/3 cup red wine vinegar

1 can (16 oz.) whole plum tomatoes,
  coarsely chopped
1 tbs. salt
3 1/2 cups diced potatoes
2 qt. beef stock
1 lb. rehydrated shredded cabbage
2 cups diced cooked beef brisket
salt and pepper to taste
sour cream for garnish
chopped fresh parsley for garnish

Heat oil and butter in a large heavy saucepan. Add onion and sauté for about 5 minutes. Add garlic, beets, celery, parsley, parsnips, sugar, vinegar, tomatoes and salt. Bring to a boil, cover, reduce heat to low and simmer for about 30 minutes. In a stockpot, simmer potatoes in stock until just tender, about 15 minutes. Add cabbage, beef and beet mixture. Bring to a boil, reduce heat to low and simmer for about 20 minutes. Season with salt and pepper. Garnish servings with sour cream and chopped parsley.

BERRIES

Use blackberries, boysenberries, huckleberries, loganberries, marionberries or raspberries.

PREPARATION: Remove stems, wash and shake dry.

PRETREATMENT: Not necessary.

DEHYDRATE: Use netted trays if small berries fall through the holes in regular trays. Dry at 100° for about 10 hours, until brittle, depending on the size of berry.

REHYDRATE: Soak in hot water for about 15 minutes; drain well.

LEATHER: Excellent for leather (see pages 141-45). Strain the seeds from the puree before drying.

NOTE
- Consider straining out the seeds before using rehydrated berries in recipes.

BERRY ICE

Use any combination of berries for this refreshing dessert or palate cleanser.

4 cups rehydrated berries
1 cup sugar, or to taste
1 tbs. lemon juice
½ cup water
fresh mint leaves for garnish

Puree berries with a blender or food processor. Strain out seeds with a sieve. Mix strained puree with sugar, lemon juice and water. Freeze according to the manufacturer's directions for your ice cream maker. Or, place in a shallow dish, cover and freeze until firm, about 2 to 3 hours. With a large spoon, scrape mixture into blender container and whirl to incorporate some air. Return to dish, cover and freeze until firm. Serve garnished with mint leaves.

BLUEBERRIES

PREPARATION: Remove stems, wash and drain.

PRETREATMENT: Checking. Drop blueberries into boiling water for 1 to 2 minutes, until skins are cracked; drain.

DEHYDRATE: Dry at 100° for about 10 hours, until leathery.

REHYDRATE: Soak in hot water for about 15 minutes; drain.

LEATHER: Blueberries are best if combined with other fruits (see pages 141-45).

NOTE
- Blueberries lose some of their aesthetic value with dehydrating, but work well for baked recipes, such as muffins or breads.

BLUEBERRY CUSTARD TARTLETS

The custard covers the rehydrated blueberries for better eye-appeal. If desired, garnish this old-fashioned treat with a dollop of sweetened whipped cream.

1 cup flour
1/4 tsp. salt
1/2 cup plus 1 tbs. chilled butter
4 oz. chilled cream cheese
4 cups rehydrated blueberries
3/4 cup sugar

2 tbs. lemon juice
1/4 tsp. ground mace or nutmeg
1/2 cup heavy cream
3 egg yolks
1/2 cup sugar
1/8 tsp. salt

In a bowl, mix flour and salt. With a pastry blender or 2 knives, cut butter and cream cheese into flour mixture until mixture appears crumbly. Form mixture into a ball, cover with plastic wrap and chill for at least 1 hour. Heat oven to 450°. Roll out dough until 1/8-inch thick. Line 8 tartlet pans with dough and crimp edges if desired. Bake for 15 minutes and remove from oven. Reduce oven heat to 375°. Drain blueberries well and gently stir in sugar, lemon juice and mace. Fill tart shells with blueberry mixture and bake for 10 minutes. Place cream, egg yolks, sugar and salt in the top part of a double boiler and cook over medium-high heat until mixture thickens, about 10 minutes, stirring frequently. Remove from heat and cool to room temperature before pouring over cooled tarts. Refrigerate until custard is set.

BROCCOLI

PREPARATION: Wash; peel the tough skin from broccoli stalks. Separate the florets from the stalks and cut stalks on the diagonal into ½-inch slices. Cut florets into uniform pieces.

PRETREATMENT: Optional. If desired, steam-blanch for about 4 minutes; drain.

DEHYDRATE: Dry at 100° for about 18 hours, until brittle.

REHYDRATE: Soak in hot water for about 30 minutes. If short on time, steam for 10 to 15 minutes, until tender. For a fresher look if planning to serve as a vegetable dish, soak in cold water for 5 minutes. Drain rehydrated broccoli before using.

NOTE
- Rehydrated broccoli is best cut up and served in a casserole dish, or pureed and mixed into custards or creamed soups.

CHICKEN AND BROCCOLI IN PHYLLO

Servings: 8

Don't let phyllo dough scare you. Once you get the knack of handling it properly, you'll find that there are many wonderful dishes you can create.

6 boneless chicken breast halves
½ cup rehydrated diced onion
1 clove garlic, minced
1 tbs. butter
½ lb. rehydrated mushrooms, finely chopped
½ cup Madeira wine
salt and pepper to taste
nutmeg to taste

1 lb. rehydrated broccoli, finely chopped
2 green onions, chopped
½ cup sour cream
¼ tsp. dried thyme
¼ tsp. dried marjoram
4 egg whites
16 sheets phyllo dough
½ cup butter, melted
Madeira Sauce, follows

Cut each chicken breast into 4 long strips. In a skillet, sauté onion and garlic in butter over medium heat until wilted. Add mushrooms and sauté for several minutes. Add Madeira and cook until moisture evaporates. Season with salt, pepper and nutmeg. In a bowl, combine broccoli with green onions, sour cream, thyme and marjoram. In another bowl, beat egg whites until soft peaks form. Fold ¼ of the egg whites into mushroom mixture and remaining egg whites into broccoli mixture.

Heat oven to 375°. Use 2 sheets of phyllo per serving; brush each piece with melted butter and stack one on top the other. Fold sheets in half lengthwise and brush again. Place 3 chicken strips across the short side of the phyllo rectangle. Top with 1/8 of each vegetable mixture. Fold the long sides of phyllo over filling and roll up into a neat package. Brush package with butter and place on a baking sheet. Repeat procedure with remaining ingredients. Bake phyllo packages for 30 minutes, or until browned. Serve topped with *Madeira Sauce*.

MADEIRA SAUCE

Makes 3 cups

1/2 cup rehydrated diced onion
1/2 cup chopped rehydrated celery
1 carrot, finely chopped
2 tbs. vegetable oil
1/4 cup butter
5 medium mushrooms, sliced
1/4 cup all-purpose flour
1 tomato, chopped

1 tbs. tomato paste
2 cups chicken stock
1/2 cup Madeira wine
1 tbs. red currant jelly
1 bay leaf
3 peppercorns
salt to taste

In a skillet, sauté onion, celery and carrot in oil and butter until golden; add mushrooms and sauté for 4 to 5 minutes. Add flour and stir well. Add remaining ingredients and simmer over low heat for 30 minutes. Strain and season.

CREAMY BAKED BROCCOLI CUSTARD

Servings: 6-8

Serve this as a vegetable side dish or as a main dish for brunch.

3-4 tbs. butter
2 cups chopped rehydrated broccoli
1 cup heavy cream
1 cup rehydrated diced onions
1 tsp. minced garlic
8 eggs

¾ cup grated Muenster or Gruyère cheese
½ cup grated Parmesan or Asiago cheese
pinch nutmeg
salt and pepper to taste

Heat oven to 375°. Heat 2 tbs. of the butter in a skillet over medium heat and sauté broccoli until soft. Transfer broccoli to a blender or food processor and process until finely minced. With machine running, gradually add cream until puree is smooth. Add remaining butter to skillet and sauté onions over medium-high heat until golden brown. Stir in garlic and remove from heat. Beat eggs in a bowl and stir in cheeses, nutmeg, salt and pepper. Stir in broccoli and onion mixtures and pour into a buttered 2-quart baking dish. Set dish in a larger dish and pour boiling water into larger dish so that it comes halfway up the sides of smaller dish. Carefully place dishes in oven and bake for 15 minutes. Reduce oven heat to 350° and bake for 40 to 45 minutes, or until a knife inserted into the center comes out clean. Let custard stand for 15 minutes before serving.

BRUSSELS SPROUTS

PREPARATION: Wash, remove tough outer leaves and cut in half.

PRETREATMENT: Steam-blanch for about 3 minutes; drain.

DEHYDRATE: Dry at 100° for about 12 to 15 hours, until brittle.

REHYDRATE: Soak in hot water for about 30 minutes. For a fresher flavor, add a little lemon juice to the soaking water. Drain before using.

NOTE
- A cheese-flavored sauce is a nice complement to Brussels sprouts' strong flavor.

BRUSSELS SPROUTS AND CARROTS IN CHEESE SAUCE

A highly flavored cheese sauce works very well with strong vegetables like Brussels sprouts. The carrots make a good color contrast and their natural sweetness balances the slightly bitter flavor of the Brussels sprouts.

2 cups rehydrated Brussels sprouts
2 cups rehydrated sliced carrots
2 cups milk
½ onion
1 bay leaf
6 whole cloves
several blades mace, or dash nutmeg
¼ cup butter
¼ cup all-purpose flour
salt and white pepper to taste
2 egg yolks
¼ cup heavy cream
¼ cup grated Parmesan cheese
¼ cup grated Gruyère cheese

Steam Brussels sprouts and carrots until just tender. Rinse with cold water and set aside. Place milk, onion, bay leaf, whole cloves and mace in a saucepan and heat until steaming. Remove from heat and let stand for about 15 minutes. Strain flavorings from milk and discard flavorings; cool. In a nonaluminum saucepan, melt butter over medium heat, add flour and stir for several minutes until flour is slightly cooked, but not browned. Add cooled milk mixture and stir with a whisk until thickened. Add salt and pepper. In a bowl, mix egg yolks with cream. Pour a little of the milk-flour mixture into yolk mixture and stir to blend. Pour yolk mixture in saucepan, stirring constantly. Add ½ of the Parmesan and Gruyère cheeses to sauce and stir until cheese is melted. Heat broiler. Place steamed vegetables in a casserole dish and cover with cheese sauce. Sprinkle remaining cheese on top. Broil until mixture is bubbly and cheese is brown.

CABBAGE, RED OR GREEN

PREPARATION: Wash, trim outer leaves, remove core and shred into ½-inch pieces.

PRETREATMENT: Steam-blanch for about 2 minutes; drain.

DEHYDRATE: Dry at 100° for about 18 hours, until crisp.

REHYDRATE: Soak in cold water with a little lemon juice for about 30 minutes; drain. Dried cabbage is usually added to soups or stews without rehydrating.

NOTE
- If you weigh the cabbage before dehydrating and label the storage container with the original weight, you can estimate the weight of the cabbage after rehydrating.
- Red cabbage will lose some of its color when rehydrated. It is best to use it in soups or stews.

SWEET AND SOUR CABBAGE

Whole books have been written on the medicinal uses of cabbage. The flavor of sweet and sour is so popular that even kids enjoy this dish. Red vinegar can be obtained through Chinese grocers. An alternative is a good balsamic or red wine vinegar to which you add some red pepper flakes or hot pepper sauce.

5 tbs. vegetable oil
1 lb. rehydrated shredded green cabbage
1 tsp. salt
1 tbs. sugar
2 tbs. red vinegar

Heat oil in a skillet or wok over high heat. Add cabbage and stir-fry until tender-crisp, about 3 minutes. Season with salt, sugar and vinegar. Stir-fry for about 30 seconds and serve immediately.

CANTALOUPE

PREPARATION: Peel, remove seeds and cut into 1/4-inch slices.

PRETREATMENT: Not necessary.

DEHYDRATE: Dry at 100° for about 33 hours, until pliable.

REHYDRATE: Soak in cold water for about 2 hours; drain.

LEATHER: Excellent for leather. You may wish to add sweeteners or mix with other fruit purees (see pages 141-45).

NOTE
- Dried cantaloupe is delicious in trail mix and is a good alternative to candy.

DRIED FRUIT TRAIL MIX

Makes 3 cups

Everyone likes trail mix. Don't limit yourself to this combination of fruit. Try at least one different fruit each time — the variations are endless.

½ cup chopped dried cantaloupe
½ cup dried banana slices
½ cup shredded coconut
½ cup mixed dried red and
    green grapes (raisins)
½ cup chopped dried dates
¼ cup chopped dried apricots,
    peaches or pears
1 cup mixed nuts, toasted, optional

Toss all ingredients together and store in an airtight container.

CARROTS

PREPARATION: Wash, trim tops and peel if desired. Cut into $1/4$-inch slices, or shred.

PRETREATMENT: Optional. Steam-blanch for about 2 minutes; drain.

DEHYDRATE: Dry at 100° for about 16 hours for slices or 12 hours for shreds, until brittle.

REHYDRATE: Soak in cold water for about 30 minutes; drain. Dried carrots can be added directly to stews and soups without rehydrating.

NOTE
- Dried carrots can be made into baby food, used in baked products or added to savory dishes like soups, casseroles and stews.

CATALINA STEW

This recipe, from my friend Tracy, adapts well to rehydrated vegetables. The secret ingredient is Catalina salad dressing, which gives the stew a rich reddish color and a tangy flavor. Stuffed green olives add the perfect balance.

2 tbs. olive oil
2 lb. beef stew meat, cut into cubes
1 cup dried diced onions
1 cup dried celery
2 cups dried sliced carrots
6 medium Yukon Gold potatoes, cut
   into 1-inch pieces

1 jar (5 oz.) small stuffed green olives
1 bottle (16 oz.) Catalina salad dressing
water to cover, plus more if necessary
1/2 tsp. pepper
salt to taste
chopped fresh parsley for garnish,
   optional

In a skillet, heat oil over medium-high heat and brown stew meat on all sides. Transfer browned meat to a crockery pot or Dutch oven. Add remaining ingredients, except parsley, using enough water to cover meat and vegetables. If using a crockery pot, cook on low for 8 hours. If using a Dutch oven, bring mixture to a boil, reduce heat to low and simmer for 2 1/2 hours or until meat is tender. Check stew halfway through cooking time and add more water if necessary. If desired, sprinkle with parsley before serving.

CARROT CAKE

Servings: 12

Carrot cake is a great way to use dehydrated carrots. If desired, sprinkle additional toasted coconut on top of cake.

3 eggs
1 cup vegetable oil
2 cups sugar
2 tsp. vanilla extract
2 cups all-purpose flour
2 tsp. cinnamon
2 tsp. baking soda

½ tsp. salt
1½ cups rehydrated shredded carrots
1 cup crushed pineapple
1 cup coconut, toasted
1 cup walnuts, toasted
Cream Cheese Frosting, follows

Heat oven to 375°. With a mixer, beat eggs, oil, sugar and vanilla until blended. In a bowl, mix flour with cinnamon, baking soda and salt and add to egg mixture. Stir in carrots, pineapple, coconut and walnuts. Pour into a greased 9-x-13-inch pan. Bake for about 50 minutes, or until cake tests done. Cool and frost with *Cream Cheese Frosting*.

CREAM CHEESE FROSTING

Makes 2 cups

3 oz. cream cheese, softened
½ cup butter, softened

1 pkg. (16 oz.) confectioners' sugar
1 tsp. vanilla extract

With a mixer, blend cream cheese with butter until smooth. Add confectioners' sugar and vanilla and beat until creamy.

CELERY

PREPARATION: Trim leaves and ends, wash and cut into ½-inch pieces.

PRETREATMENT: Soak celery pieces in a solution of 1 tbs. baking soda to 6 cups cold water for 5 minutes. Then, steam-blanch for 2 minutes; drain. Or, water-blanch celery in the soda solution for about 1 minute; drain. The soda solution helps to preserve celery's green color.

DEHYDRATE: Dry at 100° for about 18 hours, until crisp.

REHYDRATE: Soak in hot water for at least 1 hour; drain. It is not necessary to rehydrate celery before using in soups or stews.

NOTE
- To make celery flakes, chop dried celery pieces with a blender until desired texture.
- To make celery salt, mix equal parts salt with finely ground dried celery.
- If planning to grind dried celery into a powder, pretreatment is not necessary.

VEGETABLE-STUFFED SHRIMP

Rehydrated celery and onion are great in all kinds of stuffings. For this recipe, you'll need 16 large shrimp, plus ¼ lb. shrimp for the stuffing.

⅔ cup finely chopped rehydrated onion
⅔ cup finely chopped rehydrated celery
½ tsp. minced garlic
2 tbs. butter
1 cup finely chopped rehydrated mushrooms
¼ lb. shrimp, peeled and chopped

¾ cup fresh breadcrumbs
¼ cup finely chopped fresh parsley
1 egg, lightly beaten
salt and pepper to taste
16 large shrimp, peeled and deveined
3 tbs. butter, melted

Heat oven to 350°. In a skillet, sauté onion, celery and garlic in 2 tbs. butter over medium heat until wilted. Add mushrooms and sauté for about 3 minutes. Remove mixture from heat and add chopped shrimp, about ¾ of the breadcrumbs, parsley and egg. Stir to blend and season to taste. Split whole shrimp down the back about ¾ through. Open up and place flat in a buttered baking dish. Spoon equal amounts of stuffing on top of each shrimp. Sprinkle dish with remaining breadcrumbs and drizzle with 3 tbs. melted butter. Bake on lower oven rack for 2 to 3 minutes, until heated through. Heat broiler and place stuffed shrimp about 5 inches from heat source. Broil for about 5 minutes, until shrimp are nicely browned; do not overcook.

WILD RICE AND VEGETABLE PILAF

Servings: 12

This is a favorite pilaf recipe for special occasions. For an exotic flair, add a few raisins or chopped dried tomatoes.

1½ cups wild rice
1½ cups white rice
6½ cups chicken stock or water
1 lb. bacon
2 cups rehydrated diced onions
2 cups chopped rehydrated celery
½ cup chopped fresh parsley, loosely packed
¾ cup pine nuts, toasted
salt and pepper to taste

Cook rices separately, each in 3¼ cups of the stock, following package directions. Chop bacon into small pieces and sauté in a large skillet over medium-high heat until crisp. Remove bacon from skillet and drain off most of the fat. Sauté onions and celery over medium heat in skillet until tender. Add parsley, cooked rices and pine nuts. Season to taste with salt and pepper. Serve immediately.

NOTE: If you are making this ahead of time, add pine nuts just before serving.

CHERRIES

PREPARATION: Remove stems, wash and remove pits.

PRETREATMENT: Checking. Drop cherries into boiling water for 1 to 2 minutes, until skins are cracked; drain.

DEHYDRATE: Dry at 100° for about 48 to 52 hours, depending on size, until pliable with no pockets of moisture.

REHYDRATE: Soak in hot water for 15 to 20 minutes; drain.

LEATHER: Excellent for leather (see pages 141-45).

NOTE
- Dried cherries are an excellent snack food.
- Cherries look good after rehydrating and can be used in pies.
- Dried cherries can be used as a substitute for raisins in recipes.

CHERRY ALMOND CHEESE SPREAD

Servings: 12

This quick, simple appetizer spread uses cherries flavored with liqueur. If you prefer a nonalcoholic spread, eliminate the liqueur-soaking step. Add cherry, almond or orange extract to the cream cheese mixture to taste.

1 cup rehydrated dark cherries
1/2 cup amaretto or Grand Marnier liqueur
16 oz. cream cheese, softened
1 tbs. sugar, or more to taste
1 cup chopped toasted almonds
water crackers

In a bowl, cover rehydrated cherries with liqueur and refrigerate for 24 hours; drain. With a mixer, beat cream cheese until light and fluffy; add sugar, soaked cherries and almonds, if desired (almonds can also be added later). Taste and adjust sweetness. Chill mixture until firm and form into a ball. If desired, roll ball in almonds until covered. Serve with crackers.

CITRUS FRUITS AND PEELS

Use grapefruits, lemons, limes or oranges.

PREPARATION: Wash unpeeled fruit and cut into thin, even slices. If drying just the peels, use a vegetable peeler to remove the colored part of the peel; do not include the bitter white pith.

PRETREATMENT: Not necessary.

DEHYDRATE: Dry fruit at 100° for about 45 to 55 hours, until brittle. Dry peels for about 10 hours, until crisp. Fruit should be very dry before storing or it could mold.

REHYDRATE: Soak dried citrus fruits in cold water for about 2 hours; drain. Or, grind into a powder and use as a spice. It is not necessary to rehydrate dried peels, but they can also be ground into a powder and used as a spice.

LEATHER: Usually, only a small amount of citrus fruits or peels are pureed with other fruits for flavor. The natural citric acid also helps prevent discoloration (see pages 141-45).

NOTE

- Use dried citrus fruits to flavor water or punch.

CITRUS-CREAM CHEESE FILLING

Makes 2 cups

Cream cheese fillings can be used to fill rolled fruit leathers, or as a spread for tea breads, muffins or croissants.

8 oz. cream cheese, softened
1/4 cup honey, fruit juice concentrate or sugar
1 cup dried grapes (raisins) or chopped nuts
1 tbs. powdered dried citrus fruit

Mix all ingredients together. Taste and adjust sweetness.

CANDIED CITRUS PEELS

Candied citrus peels can be used to garnish desserts, or can be eaten out of hand to satisfy a sweet tooth. Avoid using fruits labeled "color added." For a treat, dip candied citrus peels in melted chocolate and place on waxed paper to dry.

2 cups rehydrated citrus peels
4½ cups cold water
1 cup sugar
½ cup water
confectioners' sugar or granulated sugar for rolling, optional

Place peels and 1½ cups of the cold water in a heavy saucepan. Bring mixture slowly to a boil, reduce heat to low and simmer for 10 minutes. Strain off water and discard. Repeat simmering process 2 more times. Transfer peels to a plate. In saucepan, bring sugar and ½ cup water to a boil, stirring until sugar dissolves. Add peels and simmer until syrup is evaporated and peels become transparent. Place candied peels in a jar and refrigerate until ready to use. Or, roll peels in sugar and place on a rack until dry, about 2 to 3 hours. Store in a tightly covered container.

CORN

PREPARATION: Shuck ears and remove silk.

PRETREATMENT: Steam-blanch ears for about 4 minutes; drain. Use a sharp knife to remove kernels.

DEHYDRATE: Dry kernels at 100° for about 18 hours, until crisp.

REHYDRATE: Soak in hot water for about 30 minutes; drain.

NOTE
- Use dried corn for soups, chowders, stews, creamed corn or casseroles.
- To make cornmeal, grind dried corn kernels with a grinder or food mill.

SHEPHERD'S PIE

Servings: 6-8

This recipe is a great way to use rehydrated vegetables. Substitute almost any diced dehydrated vegetable for variation. For an interesting flavor, use buttermilk instead of regular milk when making the mashed potatoes. If you would like it spicier, use a medium or hot salsa instead of mild.

2 lb. lean ground beef
1 cup rehydrated diced onions
⅔ cup chopped rehydrated celery
¾ cup finely chopped rehydrated carrots
2 cups rehydrated corn kernels
1½ tsp. crushed fennel seeds

2 tsp. chopped garlic
3-4 cups purchased mild tomato salsa
salt and pepper to taste
6 cups prepared mashed potatoes
1 cup shredded cheddar cheese

Heat oven to 375°. In a large skillet, cook ground beef over medium-high heat, stirring until browned and crumbly; drain off excess fat. Add onions, celery, carrots, corn, fennel seeds, garlic, salsa, salt and pepper and cook over medium heat for 10 minutes. Taste and adjust seasonings. Spoon mixture into a large, flat casserole dish. Cover with mashed potatoes and sprinkle with cheddar cheese. Bake uncovered for 20 minutes, until cheese is bubbly and mixture is hot throughout.

CORN-STUFFED ZUCCHINI

This delicious, colorful Mexican vegetable dish is easy to make.

1½ lb. fresh zucchini
2 cups rehydrated corn kernels
2 eggs
2 tbs. heavy cream
1 clove garlic, chopped
4 green onions, chopped
½ tsp. dried oregano

½ tsp. ground cumin
salt to taste
6 oz. Muenster or mild cheddar cheese, grated
3 tbs. butter, softened
purchased tomato salsa for garnish
chopped fresh cilantro to taste, optional

Heat oven to 350°. Clean and trim zucchini. Cut zucchini in half lengthwise and scoop out inner flesh, leaving a shell about ½-inch thick. Place zucchini in a buttered shallow baking dish just large enough to fit zucchini in a single layer. With a food processor or blender, blend corn, eggs, cream, garlic, green onions, oregano, cumin and salt to a coarse puree. Mix about ¾ of the cheese into puree; mixture will be quite runny. Fill zucchini shells with corn mixture. Dot with butter and sprinkle remaining cheese over the top. Cover dish with foil and bake until zucchini is tender, about 50 minutes. Serve covered with salsa, mixed with cilantro if desired.

CRANBERRIES

PREPARATION: Wash and drain.

PRETREATMENT: Checking. Drop cranberries into boiling water for 1 to 2 minutes, until skins are cracked; drain.

DEHYDRATE: Dry at 100° for about 12 hours, until leathery.

REHYDRATE: Soak in hot water for about 15 minutes; drain.

LEATHER: Cranberries are best combined with other fruits (see pages 141-45).

NOTE
- Canned cranberry sauce does not dry sufficiently to be easily removed from the trays.
- Cranberries can be used like blueberries, either dried or rehydrated before adding to baked recipes.

CRANBERRY BREAD

When cranberries are plentiful, dry a large quantity so that you can enjoy them year-round. A good spread for this bread is softened cream cheese mixed with orange juice, grated fresh orange peel (zest) and a little honey to taste.

¾ cup orange juice
1 cup dried cranberries
1 cup whole wheat flour
1 cup all-purpose flour
½ cup wheat germ
¼ tsp. salt
2 tsp. baking powder

½ tsp. baking soda
¾ cup chopped nuts
1 tbs. dried orange peel
¾ cup honey
1 egg
2 tbs. vegetable oil

Heat oven to 350°. Line a loaf pan with greased brown paper and grease sides of pan. In a saucepan, heat orange juice to boiling, remove from heat and add dried cranberries. Let berries stand for at least 15 minutes. In a bowl, combine flours, wheat germ, salt, baking powder, baking soda and nuts. In another bowl, mix together orange peel, honey, egg, oil, orange juice and cranberries until blended and add to dry mixture, stirring until just moistened. Pour batter in prepared pan and bake for 50 minutes, or until a knife inserted into the center comes out clean. Cool for 15 minutes, remove from pan and cool completely on a rack before slicing.

DATES OR FIGS

PREPARATION: Wash well. For dates, remove pits and cut in half. For figs, remove stems and cut into halves or quarters.

PRETREATMENT: Not necessary.

DEHYDRATE: Most dates in the supermarket are already sun-dried, but look for fresh ones in large open markets or import stores. Figs are easier to find and come in many varieties. The drying time varies with the type of date or fig. Dry at 100° for about 15 to 25 hours, until leathery. Lay dates and figs cut-side down on drying trays.

REHYDRATE: Not necessary.

LEATHER: Dates and figs are usually mixed with other fruit purees for additional flavor, sweetness and texture (see pages 141-45).

NOTE
- Use dried dates or figs as a snack, in baked products, in breakfast cereals, in trail mixes and in fruit compotes.

DATE SUGAR

Date sugar is sold in health food stores as an alternative to refined sugar. It is substituted in recipes as a sweetener, but cannot be used as a substitute in baking recipes where the sugar and butter are creamed, as it will not produce the proper texture. Mix date sugar with cream cheese as a spread for tea breads.

1 lb. dried dates

Cut or chop dried dates and grind into fine pieces with a food processor, food mill or blender. Spread on drying trays and dehydrate at 100° for 3 to 4 hours, until dry and not sticky. Grind to a fine powder with an electric coffee mill.

OATMEAL COCONUT DATE BARS

Makes 36

Toasting the coconut and walnuts in this bar cookie recipe creates a heavenly flavor.

4 cups rolled oats
4 cups all-purpose flour
2 cups butter, cut into pieces
2 cups brown sugar, packed
2 tsp. baking soda
2 lb. dried dates, chopped

¾ cup water
1 cup sugar, or more to taste
¼ cup lemon juice, or more to taste
2 cups walnuts, toasted
1 cup shredded coconut, toasted

Heat oven to 375°. Grease a 9-x-13-inch pan. With a pastry blender or 2 knives, mix oats, flour, butter, brown sugar and soda together until crumbly. Press ½ of the crumb mixture into prepared pan. Place remaining ingredients in a saucepan and boil until mixture thickens, about 5 minutes. Taste and add more sugar or lemon juice if desired. Pour mixture into pan and top with remaining crumb mixture. Bake for 35 minutes. Cool and cut into squares.

EGGPLANT

PREPARATION: Wash and cut into ½-inch slices.

PRETREATMENT: Not necessary. (Eggplant actually turns darker when dipped in ascorbic acid).

DEHYDRATE: Dry at 100° for about 20 hours, until leathery.

REHYDRATE: Soak in hot water for about 30 minutes; drain.

NOTE
- Dried eggplant is great to use in casseroles.
- For easy measurement, keep track of the eggplants as you dehydrate them and store them in separate, clearly labeled containers.

LAMB AND EGGPLANT CASSEROLE

Servings: 8

This is traditionally known as moussaka, and it's one of my favorite lamb dishes. This recipe takes a lot of steps to make, but it is well worth the effort!

2 lb. ground lamb
1 cup minced rehydrated onions
1/2 cup butter, optional
1/2 cup all-purpose flour
2 cups chicken stock
dash Worcestershire sauce
1/4 cup tomato paste
salt and pepper to taste

4 egg yolks, beaten
2 cups grated Monterey Jack or Swiss cheese
4 cups *White Sauce*, follows
4-6 potatoes
2 dried eggplants, rehydrated
vegetable oil

In a skillet, sauté lamb over medium-high heat until browned and crumbled. Transfer lamb to a bowl and pour off fat, reserving 1/2 cup fat if desired. Sauté onions in skillet until browned. Remove onions and add to bowl with lamb. Heat reserved lamb fat or butter over medium heat in skillet; add flour and stir for several minutes until flour is slightly cooked, but not brown. Add chicken stock and stir with a whisk until smooth. Add Worcestershire sauce, tomato paste, salt and pepper. Taste and adjust seasonings; set aside.

Stir egg yolks and 1 1/2 cups of the grated cheese into *White Sauce* and stir until cheese melts.

Peel potatoes, slice thinly and fry in a little oil or butter until golden brown. Heat broiler. Brush rehydrated eggplant with oil and broil until browned.

Heat oven to 350°. Butter a deep casserole dish and layer eggplant, meat sauce and potatoes in that order. Repeat layering and spoon white sauce over the top. Sprinkle top with remaining ½ cup cheese and bake for 30 to 40 minutes, until hot and bubbly.

WHITE SAUCE
Makes 4 cups

4 cups milk
½ small onion, cut into large chunks
few blades mace
2 slices carrot
1 bay leaf

1 sprig thyme
few parsley stalks
¼ cup butter
6 tbs. flour
salt and white pepper to taste

Place milk, onion, mace, carrot, bay leaf, thyme and parsley in a saucepan and bring almost to a boil. Cover, remove from heat and set aside for at least 15 minutes. In a heavy saucepan, melt butter over medium heat, add flour and cook for 2 to 3 minutes, allowing mixture to bubble. Strain milk mixture and add to saucepan with flour mixture, stirring constantly. Boil mixture for 2 to 3 minutes, until thickened; taste. If mixture still has a floury flavor, cook for a few more minutes. Add seasonings.

EGGPLANT CAVIAR

Eggplant caviar was the "in" food a few years back. I would like to reinstate its popularity, as it is a great all-vegetable dip for this health-conscious era.

1 dried eggplant, rehydrated
1/3 cup olive oil
3/4 cup rehydrated diced onion
2 cloves garlic, minced
1/2 cup finely chopped rehydrated green
   bell pepper
2 large tomatoes
2 tbs. balsamic vinegar

1 tsp. salt
1/2 tsp. pepper
1/2-1 tsp. sugar
sliced Greek or black olives,
   chopped green olives and/or
   capers to taste, optional
crackers or thinly sliced French bread

Chop rehydrated eggplant finely. Heat olive oil in a heavy skillet over medium heat. Add chopped eggplant, onion, garlic and green pepper. Cover and simmer for about 10 minutes. Stir in tomatoes, vinegar, salt, pepper and sugar and simmer, covered, for 10 minutes. Taste, adjust seasonings and add olives or capers if desired. Remove from heat and chill for several hours before serving. Serve with crackers.

GARLIC

PREPARATION: Use firm cloves without bruises. Peel cloves and cut in half lengthwise. Remove the green fiber that runs through the middle.

PRETREATMENT: Not necessary.

DEHYDRATE: Dry at 100° for about 6 to 8 hours, until crisp.

REHYDRATE: Soak in cold water for about 3 hours in the refrigerator; drain.

NOTE
- To make garlic powder, place dried cloves in a blender or seed grinder and process to a fine powder.
- To make garlic salt, mix 1 part garlic powder with 4 parts salt.

SWORDFISH WITH GARLIC

If swordfish is not available, use mako shark or any firm, meaty fish. Garlic is good for you, so feel free to increase the quantity.

¼ cup butter
25-30 cloves dried garlic, rehydrated
salt and pepper to taste
2 tbs. dry vermouth
4 swordfish steaks, about 1½ lb.
½ cup all-purpose flour
salt and pepper to taste
2 tbs. vegetable oil
2 tbs. butter

In a saucepan, heat ¼ cup butter over low heat and sauté garlic until cloves appear transparent and begin to brown. Add salt, pepper and vermouth and keep warm.

Rinse and dry fish. Mix flour with salt and pepper and dip fish steaks into seasoned flour mixture, coating evenly. Heat oil and butter in a skillet over medium-high heat and sauté steaks, turning once, until centers of fish are just opaque, about 10 minutes per inch of thickness. Transfer fish to a warm serving platter and spoon garlic sauce over the top. Serve immediately.

GINGER

PREPARATION: Peel fresh ginger and cut into 1/4-inch slices.

PRETREATMENT: Not necessary.

DEHYDRATE: Dry at 100° for about 18 hours, until brittle.

REHYDRATE: Soak in boiling water for 1 to 2 hours; drain.

NOTE
- To avoid waste, dehydrate the fresh ginger that is leftover after using it in a recipe.
- One tsp. rehydrated minced ginger is equal to 1/2 tsp. ground ginger.
- If you don't like to cook fish because of the way the house smells, place a few pieces of rehydrated ginger around the edges of the fish-baking dish; the room will smell of ginger instead.

CANDIED GINGER

Candied ginger is very versatile: mix it with cream cheese for an appetizer spread; cut it up and sprinkle it on ice cream; dip it in melted chocolate to satisfy a sweet tooth; or use it as a decorative garnish on desserts.

1 cup rehydrated sliced ginger
1 cup water
½ cup maple syrup

In a saucepan, simmer rehydrated ginger with water and syrup until liquid completely evaporates, about 20 minutes. Watch mixture carefully so it doesn't scorch. Remove from heat and spread on a greased drying tray, separating pieces. Dry at 100° for about 6 to 10 hours, until brittle.

GINGER ICE CREAM

This makes a fantastic dessert to serve after a spicy meal along with crisp cookies.

12 pieces dried ginger, rehydrated
1 cup sugar
4 cups heavy cream
2 tsp. vanilla extract
1/2-3/4 tsp. ground ginger
pinch salt

While the machine is running, drop rehydrated ginger pieces into a food processor or blender and process until finely minced. Add sugar and process for 1 minute, scraping down the sides of workbowl. Add remaining ingredients and stir until sugar is dissolved. Pour mixture into a 2-quart ice cream maker and freeze according to manufacturer's directions. Store in the freezer for several hours before serving, to blend flavors.

GRAPES, RED OR GREEN

PREPARATION: Use only the seedless variety. Remove grapes from stems and wash.

PRETREATMENT: Checking. Drop grapes into boiling water for several minutes, until skins are cracked; drain.

DEHYDRATE: Dry at 100° for about 80 hours, until leathery with no pockets of moisture.

REHYDRATE: Not necessary, but dried grapes (raisins) can be "plumped" if called for in the recipe by soaking in hot water for about 30 minutes.

LEATHER: Excellent for leather, especially when mixing varieties (see pages 141-45.)

NOTE

- Add dried grapes (raisins) to almost any baked product, as well as many savory dishes.
- You'll really notice a difference between the home-dried variety and the commercial brands. Save the home-dried grapes for snacks and special dishes where they will be appreciated.

RAISIN SAUCE

This is an excellent sauce for a baked ham or a pork roast. It only takes minutes to prepare, but adds so much flavor and pizzazz!

1 cup sugar
½ cup water
¾ cup chopped dried grapes (raisins)
2 tbs. butter
1 tbs. Worcestershire sauce
3 tbs. wine vinegar
½ cup red currant jelly
pinch ground mace or nutmeg
few drops Tabasco Sauce
salt and pepper to taste

In a small saucepan, boil sugar and water for 5 minutes. Add remaining ingredients, reduce heat to low and simmer, stirring, until currant jelly dissolves. Taste and adjust seasonings. Serve hot.

FRUITED HONEY BARS

Makes 16

This great, moist cookie bar is drizzled with a cinnamon glaze. For a different flavor, replace 2 tbs. of the honey with 2 tbs. molasses.

1/2 cup butter, softened
1/2 cup sugar
1/2 cup honey
1 egg
1 cup all-purpose flour
1/2 tsp. salt

1/4 tsp. cinnamon
1/8 tsp. baking soda
1/2 lb. dried dates, chopped
1/3 cup dried grapes (raisins)
1 cup chopped nuts, toasted if desired
Cinnamon Glaze, follows

Heat oven to 350°. With a mixer, beat butter, sugar, honey and egg until light and fluffy. In a separate bowl, mix flour with salt, cinnamon and soda. Beat flour mixture into butter mixture. Stir in dates, raisins and 3/4 cup of the nuts and pour into a greased and floured 9-x-9-inch pan. Bake for 45 minutes. While warm, drizzle with cinnamon glaze and sprinkle with remaining nuts.

CINNAMON GLAZE

Makes 1/2 cup

1 1/4 cups confectioners' sugar
1/4 cup hot milk

1/4 tsp. cinnamon

Mix all ingredients together until smooth.

RAISIN COOKIES

There are a million ways to use dried grapes. This is a recipe my grandmother used to make especially for me.

1 cup water
2 cups dried grapes (raisins)
1 cup butter, softened
2 cups sugar
3 eggs
1 cup chopped toasted nuts
4 cups all-purpose flour

1 tsp. baking powder
1 tsp. baking soda
2 tsp. salt
1½ tsp. cinnamon
½ tsp. ground cloves
¼ tsp. nutmeg

Heat oven to 350°. In a saucepan, pour water over dried grapes (raisins) and simmer over medium heat for 5 minutes. With a mixer, beat butter with sugar until light and fluffy. Add eggs and beat well. Mix in nuts. Mix flour, baking powder, baking soda, salt, cinnamon, cloves and nutmeg together and add to butter mixture; mix well. Drop dough by tablespoonfuls onto greased baking sheets. Bake for about 20 minutes.

KIWI FRUIT

PREPARATION: Peel and cut into 1/4-inch slices.

PRETREATMENT: Not necessary.

DEHYDRATE: Dry at 100° for 48 hours, until pliable.

REHYDRATE: Soak in hot water for about 20 minutes; drain. Kiwi fruit will lose quite a bit of color in the rehydrating process.

LEATHER: Kiwi fruit can be mixed with other pureed fruits (see pages 141-45).

NOTE
- Dried kiwi fruit is best when eaten in its dried state.
- If you choose to rehydrate, kiwi fruit can be used in baked products in the same manner as mashed bananas.

KIWI FROZEN YOGURT

The kiwi fruit in this recipe can be exchanged for other exotic dried fruits, such as papaya or mango.

¾ cup rehydrated kiwi fruit, well drained
1 tbs. lime juice
1 tbs. dried lime peel
¾ cup sugar
½ tsp. vanilla or orange extract
1 cup milk
1 cup plain yogurt
few drops green food coloring, optional

With a food processor or blender, puree kiwi fruit until smooth. Add lime juice, lime peel, sugar and vanilla; mix well. Transfer ingredients to a bowl and stir in milk, yogurt and food coloring, if using. Freeze in an ice cream maker according to manufacturer's directions. Or, place mixture in a shallow dish, cover and freeze until firm. Remove from freezer, chop into pieces and whirl in a blender or food processor to incorporate air. Return to freezer until firm. If time permits, repeat this process again for a smoother frozen yogurt.

LEEKS

PREPARATION: Remove the tough top part of leeks. Cut stalks in half lengthwise and rinse under running cold water to remove all dirt that is lodged between the layers. Cut crosswise into 1/4-inch slices and separate.

PRETREATMENT: Not necessary.

DEHYDRATE: Dry at 100° for about 18 hours, until crisp.

REHYDRATE: Soak in hot water for at least 30 minutes; drain. Dried leeks do not need to be rehydrated before adding to soups or stews.

NOTE: Dried leeks work well in cooked savory dishes like casseroles, soups and stews.

CREAMY LEEK AND BRIE SOUP

Brie gives this delicious smooth soup a rich creaminess.

½ cup butter
3 cups chopped rehydrated leeks
2 cloves garlic, minced
1½ cups rehydrated sliced mushrooms
⅓ cup all-purpose flour
1 qt. chicken or vegetable stock
2 cups half-and-half
2 tsp. dried tarragon
salt and pepper to taste
8 oz. Brie cheese, rind removed

In a stockpot, melt butter over medium heat and sauté leeks and garlic until soft. Add mushrooms and sauté until limp. Sprinkle flour over cooked vegetables and stir well. Add chicken stock and cook, stirring, until thickened. Add half-and-half, tarragon, salt and pepper. Bring soup to a gentle boil and stir in cheese until melted. Serve hot.

MANGOES

PREPARATION: Peel, remove seed and cut into $\frac{1}{4}$-inch slices.

PRETREATMENT: Not necessary.

DEHYDRATE: Dry at 100° for about 20 hours, until pliable.

REHYDRATE: Soak in cold water for about 1 hour; drain.

LEATHER: Excellent for leather (see pages 141-45).

NOTE
- Mangoes taste great in their dried form. Add them to granola, cereal or trail mix.
- If rehydrated, mangoes are best used in baked goods, cordials or chutneys.

MANGO BREAD

This delicious bread is even more tasty topped with a pineapple- or mango-flavored cream cheese spread.

2 eggs
1¼ cups sugar
¾ cup vegetable oil
2½ cups chopped rehydrated mangoes
1 tsp. lemon juice

2 cups all-purpose flour
2 tsp. cinnamon
2 tsp. baking soda
½ tsp. salt
1 cup dried grapes (raisins)

Heat oven to 350°. Line 2 loaf pans with greased brown paper and grease sides of pans. With a mixer, beat eggs. Add sugar and oil and beat until smooth. Add mangoes and lemon juice and beat well. In a bowl, mix flour with cinnamon, baking soda and salt and add to mango mixture, beating until just mixed. Stir in dried grapes (raisins) and pour batter into prepared pans. Bake for 1 hour, or until a knife inserted into the center comes out clean. Cool for 15 minutes, remove from pan and cool completely on a rack.

MUSHROOMS

PREPARATION: Rinse quickly and cut into ¼-inch slices. Mushrooms absorb water like a sponge, so work quickly.

PRETREATMENT: Not necessary.

DEHYDRATE: Dry at 100° for about 18 hours, until crisp.

REHYDRATE: Soak in cold water for about 30 minutes; drain. It is not necessary to rehydrate dried mushrooms before adding to soups or stews.

NOTE
- Dried mushrooms are excellent in spaghetti sauces, creamed dishes and all types of savory casseroles and stuffings.
- Save precious time by indicating the weight of the mushrooms before dehydrating on the storage container of dried mushrooms.

MUSHROOM BISQUE

This creamy mushroom and onion soup goes well with a thick slice of egg bread and a crisp green salad.

1/4 lb. fresh white mushrooms, sliced
1/2 cup plus 1 tbs. butter
1 tsp. lemon juice
1/2 cup finely chopped rehydrated onion
1 1/2 lb. rehydrated mushrooms, finely chopped
1 qt. chicken stock

6 tbs. all-purpose flour
3 cups milk
1 cup heavy cream
2 tsp. salt
dash Tabasco Sauce
freshly ground pepper to taste
dry sherry to taste, optional

In a skillet over medium heat, sauté fresh mushrooms in 1 tbs. butter with lemon juice until limp; set aside. In a stockpot, melt 2 tbs. of the butter and sauté onion until soft. Add rehydrated mushrooms and stir well. Add chicken stock and bring to a boil. Reduce heat to low, cover and simmer for 20 minutes. In a large skillet, heat remaining 6 tbs. butter over medium heat and add flour, stirring until blended. In a saucepan, heat milk until steaming and add to flour mixture; stir until thickened. Add mixture to stockpot and stir until smooth. Add cream, salt, Tabasco and pepper. Taste and adjust seasonings. Just before serving, swirl a small amount of sherry in each soup bowl and garnish with sautéed mushroom slices.

NECTARINES

PREPARATION: Peel, remove pit and cut into $1/4$-inch slices.

PRETREATMENT: Ascorbic acid. Soak in solution for about 2 minutes; drain.

DEHYDRATE: Dry at 100° for about 30 hours, until pliable.

REHYDRATE: Soak in hot water for about 10 minutes; drain. Nectarines tend to lose flavor and color when rehydrated.

LEATHER: Excellent for leather (see pages 141-45).

NOTE
- Dried nectarines work well for baked goods, infusions and snacks.

NECTARINE AND PEACH COBBLER

Nectarines combined with peaches add flavor and texture to this delicious old-time favorite. Serve with a scoop of ice cream or a dollop of whipped cream.

6 cups mixed rehydrated nectarines and
   peaches
1 tbs. lemon juice
1¾ cups brown sugar, packed
1 tbs. tapioca
1 tsp. apple pie spice
2 tbs. raspberry or peach liqueur
2 tbs. butter, melted

2 cups all-purpose flour
2 tsp. baking powder
½ tsp. baking soda
½ tsp. salt
½ cup butter, cut into pieces
1½ cups buttermilk
2 tbs. granulated sugar
½ tsp. cinnamon

Heat oven to 425°. Place nectarines and peaches in a greased 9-x-13-inch pan and sprinkle with lemon juice. Stir in brown sugar, tapioca, apple pie spice and liqueur and drizzle with melted butter. In a bowl, combine flour, baking powder, soda and salt. With a pastry blender or 2 knives, cut ½ cup butter into flour mixture until pieces are the size of peas. Stir in buttermilk until just mixed. Drop batter by tablespoonfuls onto nectarine and peach mixture, leaving some space between batter portions. Mix sugar and cinnamon together and sprinkle over cobbler batter. Bake for 30 minutes, until golden brown. Serve warm.

NECTARINE CORDIAL

Cordials are generally served as an after-dinner drink. They make great home-made gifts.

1 lb. dried nectarines
2 cups sugar
1 cup brandy
3½ cups dry white wine

Place all ingredients in a sterilized glass jar and stir until sugar dissolves. Cover tightly and let stand at room temperature in a dark place for at least 1 week. Swirl mixture occasionally. Remove fruit when it appears to be turning mushy, usually after about 4 weeks. Strain mixture, discard fruit and transfer cordial to sterilized decorative bottles. Label bottles clearly.

ONIONS

PREPARATION: Remove papery shell, dice or cut into 1/4-inch slices.

PRETREATMENT: Not necessary.

DEHYDRATE: Dry at 100° for about 20 hours, until brittle.

REHYDRATE: Soak in hot water for about 15 minutes; drain. It is not necessary to rehydrate dried onions before adding to soups or stews.

NOTE
- Add dried onions to hot savory dishes.
- Be aware that dehydrating onions will make the house smell strongly.
- To make onion flakes or powder, place dried onions in a blender, grinder or food mill and process until ground to desired size.
- To make onion salt, mix equal parts salt with finely ground onion powder.

FISH CHOWDER

Servings: 6

This rich, creamy chowder, made from several varieties of rehydrated vegetables, takes only minutes to prepare. Serve with a crisp green salad and hearty bread.

1/3 cup butter
1/4 cup rehydrated diced green bell pepper
1 cup rehydrated diced onions
2 cups rehydrated diced potatoes, prefer Yukon Gold
1 cup rehydrated sliced mushrooms
2 lb. snapper fillets, cubed
1 1/2 cups rehydrated corn kernels

2 cans (10 3/4 oz. each) condensed cream of mushroom soup
2 cups half-and-half
1/4 cup dry white wine
1 tsp. pepper
salt to taste
1 jar (4 oz.) diced pimientos, drained
finely chopped fresh parsley for garnish, optional

Melt butter over medium heat in a heavy large saucepan or Dutch oven. Add green pepper, onions, potatoes and mushrooms and sauté for about 5 minutes. Add fish and corn and sauté for 10 minutes. In a bowl, combine mushroom soup, half-and-half and wine. Whisk until smooth and add to saucepan. Cook, stirring, until mixture is heated through. Stir in pepper, salt and pimiento, taste and adjust seasonings. If desired, sprinkle with parsley and serve immediately.

ONION SALAD DRESSING

Using this as a base recipe, you can substitute different flavors of vinegar, such as balsamic or tarragon. This recipe can also be used as a marinade for meat or poultry.

1 cup rehydrated diced white onions
2 tsp. chopped rehydrated garlic, or
    2 cloves fresh garlic, chopped
1½ cups olive oil or other oil
⅔ cup white wine vinegar
3 tbs. sugar
1 tsp. dry mustard
1 tsp. salt

Place all ingredients in a blender container and process until thoroughly mixed. Keep refrigerated until ready to serve. Keeps refrigerated for 3 to 4 weeks.

PAPAYAS

PREPARATION: Peel, halve, remove seeds and cut into $1/4$-inch strips.

PRETREATMENT: Not necessary.

DEHYDRATE: Dry at 100° for about 20 hours, until pliable.

REHYDRATE: Soak in cold water for at least 1 hour; drain.

LEATHER: Excellent for leather, especially when combined with other fruit purees (see pages 141-45).

NOTE
- Dried papaya is good for snacking, but tends to be mushy when rehydrated.
- Dried papaya is delicious in sorbets and frozen yogurts.

MIXED FRUIT SOUP

Servings: 8

Serve this as a refreshing starter or a delicious dessert. You can create a totally different taste by changing the combination of dried fruits used.

2 cups water
2 slices dried or fresh lemon
2 slices dried or fresh orange
1/4 tsp. cinnamon
pinch ground cloves
2 cups chopped mixed papayas and
   other fruits
1 cup water
2 cups orange juice

1 tbs. lemon juice
1 cup canned pineapple chunks
   with juice
1/4 cup honey, or more to taste
dash salt
2 tbs. tapioca
whipped cream or flavored yogurt for
   garnish, optional
ice cream or frozen yogurt, optional

Combine 2 cups water, lemon slices, orange slices, cinnamon, cloves and mixed dried fruit in a saucepan and bring to a boil. Cover, remove from heat and let stand for about 30 minutes. In another saucepan, combine 1 cup water, orange juice, lemon juice, pineapple, honey, salt and tapioca. Drain rehydrated fruit and remove and discard lemon and orange slices. Add remaining fruit to orange juice mixture. Bring to a boil, reduce heat to low and simmer for 15 minutes. Taste and adjust sweetness. Serve hot or chilled, garnished with a dollop of whipped cream if desired. Or, serve soup over ice cream.

PARSNIPS

PREPARATION: Wash, peel and cut into ¼-inch slices or shred.

PRETREATMENT: Steam-blanch for about 4 minutes; drain.

DEHYDRATE: Dry sliced parsnips at 100° for about 16 to 18 hours, until brittle; dry shredded parsnips for 10 to 12 hours.

REHYDRATE: Soak in hot water for at least 1 hour; drain.

NOTE
- Parsnips are wonderful mashed, or added to cream sauces, stews and casseroles.

PUREED PARSNIPS

Parsnips as a general rule are overlooked vegetables, but they have a wonderful, natural sweet flavor. I like to serve these as an alternative to mashed potatoes or stuffed into a steamed vegetable like zucchini.

2 lb. dried parsnips
water to cover
6-8 tbs. heavy cream
2 tbs. butter
salt and pepper to taste
nutmeg to taste

In a saucepan, cover parsnips with water and bring to a boil. Reduce heat to medium and cook until very tender, about 15 to 20 minutes; drain well. Transfer parsnips to a vegetable mill or food processor and process until smooth. Beat in cream, butter and seasonings. Transfer mixture to the top of a double boiler and simmer, covered, for about 25 minutes. The texture and flavor changes considerably with additional cooking. Correct seasonings before serving.

PEACHES

PREPARATION: Wash, dip into boiling water for about 30 to 60 seconds and plunge into cold water. Remove skins. Halve peeled peaches, remove pits and cut into ¼-inch slices.

PRETREATMENT: Ascorbic acid. Soak in solution for for 2 to 3 minutes; drain.

DEHYDRATE: Dry at 100° for about 30 hours, until pliable.

REHYDRATE: Soak in cold water for 1 hour, or in hot water for 15 minutes; drain.

LEATHER: Excellent for leather (see pages 141-45). Reduce drying time to about 14 hours.

NOTE
- Dried peaches are good for baked goods, such as pies and cobblers.
- Try dried peaches in chutney, cereal, trail mix, ice cream, frozen yogurt and sorbet.

GINGER PEACH JAM

If you have a large quantity of dried peaches on hand, consider turning it into a delicious jam. Increase the amount of candied ginger if you like a spicier jam. This can be spooned over cream cheese and served with crackers for an interesting hors d'oeuvre.

3¾ cups rehydrated peaches
¼ cup lemon juice
about ¼ cup finely chopped candied ginger, or to taste
1 pkg. (1¾ oz.) powdered pectin
5 cups sugar

Chop rehydrated peaches and place in a large saucepan. Add lemon juice, candied ginger and pectin; stir well. Place over high heat and bring quickly to a boil, stirring constantly. Add sugar, continue stirring and bring back to a full boil. Boil for about 1 minute, stirring constantly. Remove from heat. Fill sterilized canning jars with jam, leaving a ⅛-inch space at the top. Secure canning lids. Submerge jam-filled jars in boiling water for about 5 minutes. Remove jars from water and cool for at least 12 hours. Check lids for a proper seal by pressing the center. If the lid springs up, reprocess jam with a new lid before cooling. Store jam in a cool, dark place.

PEARS

PREPARATION: Peel, core and cut into 1/4-inch slices.

PRETREATMENT: Ascorbic acid. Soak in solution for 2 to 3 minutes; drain.

DEHYDRATE: Dry at 100° for about 10 hours, until pliable.

REHYDRATE: Soak in cold water for 20 minutes; drain.

LEATHER: Excellent for leather (see pages 141-45). Add 1 tsp. ascorbic acid for every 3 pears. Pear leather will have a brown color, but the flavor is excellent.

NOTE
- Dried pears are great for snacks, or in baked products, cereal, trail mix and chutney.

MIXED FRUIT COFFEECAKE

You can add almost any combination of dried fruits to this cake batter to create a different look and flavor. If you use a lot of dried cherries, consider using almond or cherry extract instead of vanilla extract.

1½ cups mixed dried pears and other
   fruits
boiling water
2 cups all-purpose flour
2 tsp. baking powder
¼ tsp. salt
¾ cup butter, softened
¾ cup sugar
1 tsp. vanilla or other flavor extract

2 eggs
¾ cup milk
1 cup dark brown sugar, packed
1 tbs. all-purpose flour
1 tbs. cinnamon
½ cup chopped nuts
¼ cup butter, melted
confectioners' sugar

Continued on the next page

Heat oven 350°. Cover dried fruits with boiling water and let stand for about 15 minutes; drain well and chop finely. Mix together 2 cups flour, baking powder and salt. With a mixer, beat butter and sugar until light and fluffy. Add vanilla and eggs and beat well. Add milk to creamed butter mixture alternately with flour mixture. Stir in chopped fruits. Combine brown sugar, 1 tbs. flour, cinnamon and chopped nuts. Spoon ⅓ of the batter into a greased and floured tube pan and sprinkle with ½ of the brown sugar mixture. Drizzle ½ of the melted butter over the top and repeat process. Top with remaining batter, spreading the top smoothly. Bake for about 1 hour, or until a knife inserted into cake comes out clean. Cool for 15 minutes before removing from pan. Cool completely and sprinkle with confectioners' sugar.

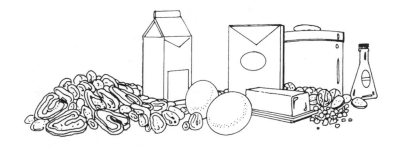

PEAS

PREPARATION: Shell.

PRETREATMENT: Steam-blanch for 3 minutes; drain.

DEHYDRATE: Dry at 100° for about 12 hours, until shriveled and brittle.

REHYDRATE: Soak in hot water for about 30 minutes; drain.

NOTE
- Peas are good mixed into hot savory dishes like stews, soups and casseroles.

RICE AND PEAS WITH SHRIMP

Servings: 6

This was served to me by a wonderful Italian cook — it is a nice alternative to potatoes. Consider serving it at a luncheon with homemade rolls, a green salad and a fruit dessert. Check your supermarket's gourmet section for arborio rice.

1/4 cup olive oil
1/4 cup butter
1/2 cup minced rehydrated onion
1 1/2 cups arborio rice
3 tbs. dry white wine
about 3 cups chicken stock
1 tsp. salt

1 1/2 cups rehydrated peas
3/4 lb. shrimp, peeled, deveined and cooked
1 clove garlic, minced
2 tbs. butter
1/4 cup grated Parmesan cheese

Heat oil and butter in a saucepan over medium heat and sauté rehydrated onion for about 5 minutes. Mix in rice and sauté until rice appears translucent. Add wine and cook for 1 minute. Add 1 1/2 cups of the stock and salt and cook, stirring, until stock is absorbed. Add peas and 1 cup of the stock, cooking until absorbed. Rice should be tender, but slightly firm to the bite, *al dente*. Repeat process with a small amount of stock if needed. Sauté shrimp and garlic in 2 tbs. butter over medium heat just until warmed through. Reserve 6 shrimp for garnish and add remaining mixture to rice. Add Parmesan and mix gently, adding more stock if mixture appears too dry. Garnish each serving with 1 shrimp.

PASTA CARBONARA

This traditional Italian favorite combines bacon, garlic and peas. Serve it with homemade breadsticks and salad.

2 lb. bacon, diced
1½ lb. dried spaghetti, fettuccine or
   other pasta
½ cup butter
3 cloves garlic, minced
4 eggs, beaten

½ tsp. red pepper flakes
⅓ cup grated Romano cheese
¾ cup grated Parmesan cheese
1 cup rehydrated peas
½ cup coarsely chopped Greek or black
   olives, optional

In a large skillet, sauté bacon over medium-high heat until crisp; drain on paper towels and discard fat. Cook pasta according to package directions until slightly firm to the bite, *al dente*. Rinse with cold water and drain. Heat butter in skillet over medium heat, add garlic and cook slightly; do not brown. Add cooked pasta and toss well. In a bowl, mix eggs with pepper flakes, 2 tbs. of the Romano cheese and 2 tbs. of the Parmesan cheese. Pour cheese mixture over pasta and toss to mix. Cook, stirring, for several minutes, until slightly thickened. Just before serving, add peas and bacon. Sprinkle with remaining cheese and olives, if using, and serve immediately.

PEPPERS, BELL (GREEN OR RED)

PREPARATION: Wash, remove seeds and ribs, dice or cut into $1/4$-inch slices.

PRETREATMENT: Not necessary.

DEHYDRATE: Dry at 100° for about 24 hours, until brittle.

REHYDRATE: Soak in hot water for at least 20 minutes; drain.

NOTE
- Dried bell peppers work well in cooked savory dishes, such as soups, stews or casseroles.
- Add dried bell peppers to tossed salads for extra crunch.

LEMON TAHINI DRESSING

Makes 2½ cups

This is a great way to use several different varieties of dehydrated vegetables. Use this dressing on salads or as a sauce for grains, such as brown rice. Tahini is a paste made from sesame seeds, and can be found in health food stores, gourmet shops and some supermarkets. You can substitute smooth peanut butter for a slightly different flavor.

1 cup vegetable oil
¼ cup lemon juice, or more to taste
¼ cup tamari or soy sauce
¼ cup chopped rehydrated green bell pepper
¼ cup chopped rehydrated onion
¼ cup chopped rehydrated celery
½ cup toasted sesame tahini

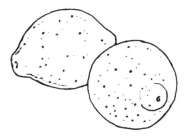

Blend all ingredients with a blender or food processor until smooth. Taste and add more lemon juice if desired. Store in a covered jar in the refrigerator. Keeps for about 2 weeks.

VEGETABLE-STUFFED BRIE

Servings: 24

This is a delicious and colorful appetizer that can be served year-round, but is ideal for Christmas if you use dried red and green bell peppers. Serve with a crusty French bread.

2 cloves garlic, minced
½ cup rehydrated diced onion
1 tbs. butter
8 large white mushrooms, finely chopped
½ cup mixed rehydrated diced red and
   green bell peppers

1 cup sliced black or Greek olives
1 tbs. dry sherry or white wine
dash salt and pepper
1 large wheel Brie cheese, sliced in half
   horizontally
sliced French bread

In a small skillet, sauté garlic and onion in butter over medium heat until tender. Add mushrooms, peppers and olives and sauté for 3 minutes. Add sherry and season to taste. Cool.

About 1 hour before serving, spread all but ¾ cup of the filling on the bottom half of Brie. Place top half of Brie over filling. Sprinkle remaining ¾ cup filling on top of Brie. Serve with French bread slices.

SEAFOOD AND RED PEPPER MOUSSE

This wonderful, rich mousse makes an elegant appetizer. Garnish the top with a bit of the chosen seafood and chopped fresh parsley.

2 tbs. unflavored gelatin
1/4 cup cold water
1 cup boiling water
3/4 cup rehydrated sliced red bell pepper
1 small red onion, chopped
1 cup mayonnaise
1/4 tsp. cayenne pepper
1 tbs. lemon juice

1 cup heavy cream
2 cups mixed cooked seafood, such as crab, lobster, shrimp or white fish cut into pieces
salt to taste
assorted crackers
curly leaf lettuce or lemon wedges for garnish

Heat broiler. Dissolve gelatin in cold water. Add boiling water and chill until syrupy. Broil rehydrated red peppers until slightly brown. Process red peppers and onion with a food processor or blender until pureed. Add mayonnaise and chilled gelatin and blend. Fold in cayenne and lemon juice. Whip cream until stiff and fold into bell pepper mixture. Add seafood and fold into mixture. Taste and adjust seasonings. Pour mixture into an oiled 6-cup mold and chill for at least 4 hours or overnight. Unmold mousse onto a serving plate garnished with lettuce leaves or lemon wedges. Serve with assorted crackers.

PINEAPPLE

PREPARATION: Wash, peel, core and cut into $\frac{1}{2}$-inch slices.

PRETREATMENT: Not necessary.

DEHYDRATE: Dry at 100° for about 72 hours, until leathery, but not sticky. Drying time can vary greatly depending on the size of slices.

REHYDRATE: Soak in hot water for about 15 minutes; drain.

LEATHER: Excellent for leather (see pages 141-45).

NOTES
- Dried pineapple is most often used in its dried state. It's great in baked goods and candies, or as a snack.
- It is important to remember not to use fresh or rehydrated pineapple in gelatin recipes because the acid in the pineapple will prevent the gelatin from setting.

PINEAPPLE-MACADAMIA NUT BREAD

Macadamia nuts and pineapple are a great combination. You can give this even more tropical flair by adding about 1/2 cup dried coconut.

1 1/2 cups sugar
1/2 cup butter, softened
3 eggs
1 tsp. vanilla extract
1/2 cup pineapple juice

3 cups all-purpose flour
1 1/2 tsp. baking powder
1/2 tsp. salt
1 cup chopped macadamia nuts
1 cup chopped dried pineapple

Heat oven to 350°. Line the bottom of a loaf pan with greased brown paper and grease sides of pan. With a mixer, beat sugar and butter until light and fluffy. Add eggs one at a time, mixing well after each addition. Add vanilla and pineapple juice and mix well. Mix flour, baking powder and salt together and stir into butter mixture. Stir in nuts and pineapple. Pour batter into prepared pan and bake for 1 to 1 1/4 hours, until a knife inserted into the center of bread comes out clean. Cool for 15 minutes in pan, remove from pan and cool completely on a rack.

PLUMS

PREPARATION: Rinse, halve and remove pits. Flatten plum halves by pressing them between your hands. Or, cut halves into 1/4-inch slices.

PRETREATMENT: Not necessary.

DEHYDRATE: Dry halved plums at 100° for about 72 hours. Dry sliced plums at 100° for about 30 to 35 hours. Dried plums (prunes) should be leathery with no pockets of moisture.

REHYDRATE: Optional. Soak in cold water for about 2 hours; drain. Or, soak in hot water or fruit juice for about 10 minutes; drain. You can also steam prunes for about 5 minutes; drain.

LEATHER: Dried plums (prunes) work well for leather, but you may wish to mix them with other fruit purees because of their laxative effect (see pages 141-45).

NOTES

- Dehydrating 2 1/2 lb. fresh plums yields about 1 lb. dried plums (prunes).
- Use dried plums in both sweet and savory dishes.

WILD RICE STUFFING

The spices and dried fruit give this stuffing an exotic flavor. Serve with all forms of poultry and wild game dishes.

1½ cups minced rehydrated onions
¾ cup diced rehydrated celery
¼ cup butter
12 peppercorns
6 whole cloves
4 inch cinnamon stick
¼ tsp. ground cardamom, or 6 whole cardamom pods
2 cloves garlic

3½ cups chicken stock
1 cup wild rice
salt and pepper to taste
1 cup white rice
1 cup dried green grapes (raisins)
¼ cup diced dried apricots
½ cup dried plums (prunes)
½ cup slivered almonds, toasted

In a saucepan over medium heat, sauté onions and celery in butter until wilted. Place peppercorns, cloves, cinnamon stick, cardamom and garlic in a small square of cheesecloth and tie securely with kitchen string. Hit spices with a mallet until crushed and add to saucepan with chicken stock, wild rice, salt and pepper. Bring to a boil, reduce heat to low, cover and simmer for 30 minutes. Add white rice, raisins, apricots and prunes; cover and simmer for 15 minutes. Remove spice bag and lightly mix in toasted almonds. Taste and adjust seasonings.

PRUNE NUT CAKE

Servings: 12

This is a very moist, delicious cake. Next time, instead of prunes, use dried chopped dates with a little cinnamon for a great new taste sensation.

2 cups cake flour
1 cup sugar
¼ cup unsweetened cocoa powder
2 tbs. baking powder
¼ tsp. salt
1 lb. rehydrated plums (prunes),
   liquid reserved and chilled
1 cup chopped toasted nuts
1 cup mayonnaise
1 cup cold water, optional
1 tsp. vanilla extract

Heat oven to 350°. Sift flour, sugar, cocoa, baking powder and salt together. Stir in rehydrated plums (prunes) and chopped nuts. Mix mayonnaise with 1 cup of the reserved plum liquid or water and vanilla. Stir mayonnaise mixture into flour mixture and blend thoroughly. Pour into a greased 9-x-13-inch pan. Bake for about 35 minutes, or until cake springs back to the touch. Cool and cut into squares.

POTATOES

PREPARATION: Scrub, peel and rinse. Dice, grate or cut into ¼-inch slices.

PRETREATMENT: Ascorbic acid or citric acid. Soak in ascorbic acid solution or lemon juice for about 5 minutes; drain.

DEHYDRATE: Dry at 100° for about 8 hours, until crisp.

REHYDRATE: Soak in cold water for about 30 minutes; drain and pat dry.

NOTE
- Without pretreatment, potatoes will turn black.
- Dried potatoes are great for layered potato dishes, such as scalloped potatoes, or added to casserole dishes.
- To easily convert recipes that call for potatoes by the pound, weigh the potatoes before dehydration and note the original weight on the storage container.

POTATO VARIATIONS

MASHED POTATOES: Cover diced, grated or sliced potatoes with boiling water and let stand for 20 minutes. Test with a fork for tenderness. If needed, boil in water until potatoes are very tender and drain off water. Place cooked potatoes in a blender container and blend until mashed. Add hot milk or cream, melted butter and salt to taste. If desired, add a sprinkling of grated cheese.

ROASTED GARLIC MASHED POTATOES: Heat oven to 375°. Cut about ½ inch off the top of a garlic bulb, leaving bulb intact. Rub bulb with olive oil and place in a baking dish with a little water. Cover dish with foil and bake for about 45 minutes. Remove foil and bake for about 10 minutes, until garlic browns slightly. Garlic cloves should be soft enough to squeeze from their skins like a paste. Blend garlic paste with mashed potatoes to taste.

HASH BROWNS: Rehydrate the desired amount of grated potatoes (see page 119). Add rehydrated diced onions to taste and, if desired, rehydrated red or green bell peppers. Season with salt and pepper. Heat butter or bacon drippings in a skillet and sauté potatoes over medium-high heat until browned on both sides and heated through.

CLAM CHOWDER

This simple chowder is a great way to use dehydrated potatoes. Serve it with cornbread and a Caesar salad.

3 cans (10¾ oz. each) minced clams
water
½ lb. lean salt pork or bacon, diced
1 cup rehydrated diced onions
3 cups rehydrated diced potatoes
1 tsp. salt

¼ tsp. white pepper
2 cups half-and-half
2 cups milk
2 tbs. butter
½ tsp. thyme, optional
paprika for garnish

Strain clams and reserve liquid. Measure clam liquid and add water to make 4 cups liquid. Sauté salt pork over medium-high heat in a large saucepan until golden. Remove pork and drain on paper towels. Discard all but ¼ cup of the fat. Add onions to pan and sauté for 5 minutes. Add potatoes, salt, pepper and clam liquid and bring to a boil. Reduce heat to low and simmer until potatoes are tender, about 15 minutes. Add clams, cream, milk, butter and thyme, if using. Cook until heated through, but do not boil. Sprinkle with paprika before serving.

POTATO CHEESE BAKE

This is an easy, good dish to serve with roasted meats and poultry and a crisp green vegetable.

1½ lb. rehydrated sliced potatoes
3 cloves garlic, minced
4 oz. Gruyère or Swiss cheese, shredded
salt and white pepper to taste
nutmeg to taste
2 cups chicken stock

Heat oven to 400°. Layer potatoes with garlic, cheese and seasonings in a well-buttered casserole dish. Pour chicken stock over potatoes, cover and bake for 30 minutes. Remove cover and bake for about 15 minutes, or until potatoes are fork-tender.

RADISHES

PREPARATION: Wash, trim and cut into ¼-inch slices.

PRETREATMENT: Not necessary.

DEHYDRATE: Dry at 100° for about 15 hours, until crisp.

REHYDRATE: Soak in cold water for about 30 minutes; drain.

NOTE
- Dried radishes add spiciness to cooked dishes.
- Toss dried radishes into salads for spiciness and crunch.
- Mix rehydrated radishes into cream cheese as a dip for crudités.

SWEET AND SOUR RADISH SALAD

Radishes lose a little color and texture when rehydrated. Mixing them with a marinade, salad dressing or light sauce helps to disguise them.

1½ cups rehydrated radishes
salt to taste
3 tbs. sugar
3 tbs. balsamic vinegar
1 tbs. light soy sauce
2 tbs. sesame oil
toasted sesame seeds for garnish, optional

In a bowl, sprinkle radishes with salt and let stand for about 20 minutes. Mix sugar with vinegar, soy sauce and sesame oil, pour over salted radishes and toss well. Taste and adjust seasonings. Chill. If desired, sprinkle with toasted sesame seeds just before serving.

RHUBARB

PREPARATION: Wash, trim and slice stalks into 1-inch pieces. Do not use the leaves, as they are poisonous.

PRETREATMENT: Optional. To guarantee tenderness, steam-blanch rhubarb for 1 to 2 minutes; drain.

DEHYDRATE: Dry at 100° for about 12 hours, until crisp.

REHYDRATE: Soak in cold water for about 1 hour; drain. If using as a filling or sauce, place in a saucepan, cover with hot water and simmer until just tender.

LEATHER: Because rhubarb is very tart, it should be mixed with other sweet fruit purees, such as strawberries or apples (see pages 141-45).

NOTE
- Rhubarb has a tendency to lose color after drying, but also tends to be less tart.

RHUBARB CREAM CHEESE PIE

My sister Karen gave me this recipe. We went to a church pie social together and I liked her pie the best.

one 9-inch pastry crust, unbaked
4 cups rehydrated rhubarb
3 tbs. cornstarch
1/4 tsp. salt
1 1/2 cups sugar, or more to taste

8 oz. cream cheese, softened
2 eggs
1/2 tsp. vanilla extract
1 cup sour cream
sliced almonds for garnish

Heat oven to 425°. Line a 9-inch pie pan with pastry. In a heavy saucepan, cook rhubarb, cornstarch, salt and 1 cup of the sugar over medium heat until mixture boils and thickens. Cool and pour into pan. Bake for 10 minutes and remove from oven. With a mixer, beat cream cheese, eggs, remaining 1/2 cup sugar and vanilla until smooth. Pour over rhubarb mixture. Reduce oven heat to 350° and bake pie for 30 minutes, or until topping is set. Cool and chill. Spread sour cream over chilled pie and garnish with sliced almonds before serving.

RHUBARB RELISH

My dear friend's mother, Myrtle, gave me this recipe. This sauce is a great accompaniment to beef, pork or poultry.

2 cups rehydrated rhubarb
1 cup cider vinegar
2 cups rehydrated diced onions
1 pkg. (16 oz.) dark brown sugar
1 tsp. celery seeds
½ tsp. cinnamon
½ tsp. salt
½ tsp. pepper
1½ tsp. ground cloves

In a heavy saucepan, mix rhubarb with vinegar and bring to a boil. Reduce heat to low and simmer for about 20 minutes. Add remaining ingredients and simmer for about 1 hour, until thick. Taste and adjust sweetness or spices.

SPINACH

PREPARATION: Wash well and remove stems.

PRETREATMENT: Not necessary.

DEHYDRATE: Dry at 100° for about 10 to 12 hours, until brittle.

REHYDRATE: Soak in hot water for about 15 minutes; drain. Adding a little lemon juice to the soaking water can freshen the flavor.

NOTE
- Always squeeze spinach dry before using in recipes.

SPINACH QUICHE

Serve this for breakfast or lunch. If you wish to add meat, add ½ cup cooked bacon pieces or chopped ham with the cheese.

one 9-inch pastry crust, unbaked
½ cup shredded Gruyère cheese
1 tbs. butter
2 tbs. rehydrated diced onion
1 cup rehydrated spinach, squeezed dry
dash nutmeg

6 eggs, lightly beaten
1 cup sour cream
1 cup milk
½ tsp. salt
⅛ tsp. pepper

Heat oven to 400°. Line a 9-inch pie pan with pastry and sprinkle with cheese. Heat butter in a skillet over medium heat and sauté onion until wilted. Stir in spinach and nutmeg. Remove from heat and cool mixture slightly. In a bowl, beat eggs with sour cream, milk, salt and pepper. Spoon spinach mixture over cheese in pan and pour egg mixture over the top. Bake for 10 minutes, reduce oven heat to 325° and bake until custard is set, about 30 minutes. Serve warm.

STRAWBERRIES

PREPARATION: Wash, hull and cut into ¼-inch slices.

PRETREATMENT: Not necessary.

DEHYDRATE: Dry at 100° for about 30 hours, until leathery.

REHYDRATE: Soak in hot water for about 15 minutes; drain. Strawberries will become mushy if left to soak for too long. Dried strawberries can be added directly to recipes without rehydrating unless the recipe calls for mashed fruit.

LEATHER: Excellent for leather, alone or mixed with other fruit purees (see pages 141-45).

NOTE
- Use dried strawberries for snacks, in cereal, such as granola, and in dairy products, such as ice cream, milk shakes and yogurt.

STRAWBERRY GRANOLA

Add almost any type of dried fruit to this delicious recipe.

4 cups old-fashioned oats
1 cup sunflower kernels
1/2 cup sesame seeds
1 cup dried coconut
1/4 cup wheat germ
1/2 cup bran flakes
1/2 cup soy grits, optional
1 1/2 cups cashew nuts or peanuts

1/4 cup powdered milk (do not use instant)
3/4 cup vegetable oil
1/2 cup brown sugar, packed
3/4 cup honey
1 tsp. vanilla extract
1-2 cups chopped dried strawberries or other fruit

Heat oven to 275°. Mix oats with sunflower kernels, sesame seeds, coconut, wheat germ, bran flakes, soy grits, nuts and powdered milk. Mix oil with brown sugar, honey and vanilla and toss with oat mixture. Transfer to a large greased baking pan and bake for about 1 hour, stirring every 15 minutes, until mixture turns golden brown. Remove from oven, add dried strawberries and spread out on waxed paper until cooled. Use your hands to crumble into smaller pieces.

TOMATOES

PREPARATION: Wash and remove stems. For beefsteak tomatoes, cut into ½-inch slices. For plum tomatoes, slice in half lengthwise. Remove seeds if desired.

PRETREATMENT: Not necessary.

DEHYDRATE: Dry beefsteak tomatoes at 100° for about 24 hours, until crisp. Place plum tomatoes cut-side down on tray and dry at 100° for 72 hours, until crisp.

REHYDRATE: Soak beefsteak tomatoes in cold water for about 15 minutes; drain. Soak plum tomatoes in cold water for at least 30 minutes; drain.

NOTE

- Dried beefsteak tomatoes work well in sauces, stews and casseroles.
- Dried plum tomatoes are great for marinating and using in pasta dishes, salads or casseroles.

MARINATED "SUN-DRIED" TOMATOES

Makes about ¼ pound

Dehydrated plum tomatoes are the next best things to sun-dried tomatoes and make great marinated tomatoes, which can be used in pasta dishes, salads, pizzas, omelets or other savory hot dishes.

1 lb. dried plum tomatoes
1 tsp. dried basil
1 tsp. minced garlic
pepper to taste
6 juniper berries, or 1 sprig rosemary, optional
olive oil

Pack dried tomatoes, basil, garlic, pepper and juniper berries, if using, in a large glass jar. Cover with olive oil, seal well and refrigerate for about 1 month. When ready to use, let jar stand at room temperature until olive oil clears and becomes liquidy. Drain off olive oil and cut tomatoes into strips with scissors or a knife. You can use the flavored olive oil in salad dressings or to flavor pasta dishes.

LAMB STEW

This particular stew has a Middle Eastern flair, and, following tradition, I like to serve it over steamed couscous. You may prefer rice.

2 tbs. vegetable oil
1½ lb. lamb stew meat, cut into cubes
1 medium onion, chopped
2 cups rehydrated tomatoes
2 cloves garlic, minced
1 tsp. ground ginger
1 tsp. fennel seeds, optional
1 tsp. hot pepper sauce, or to taste

1 tsp. turmeric
½ cup canned garbanzo beans
1½ cups water
2 carrots
1 zucchini
6-8 small new potatoes
salt and pepper to taste
steamed couscous or rice

Heat oil in a heavy large saucepan over medium heat and add lamb and onion. Cook, stirring, for about 15 minutes. Dice tomatoes and add to meat mixture with garlic, ginger, fennel seeds, hot pepper sauce, turmeric, garbanzo beans and water. Bring to a boil, reduce heat to low and simmer for 1 hour. Cut carrots and zucchini into large chunks. Leave potatoes whole or cut into smaller pieces. Add vegetables to stew and simmer for about 20 minutes, until vegetables are tender. Add salt and pepper to taste. Serve over steamed couscous.

WATERMELON

PREPARATION: Remove rind and seeds. Cut flesh into ¼-inch slices.

PRETREATMENT: Not necessary.

DEHYDRATE: Dry at 100° for about 33 hours, until pliable.

REHYDRATE: Soak in cold water for about 1 hour; drain. Watermelon tends to be mushy when rehydrated.

LEATHER: Not recommended for leather.

NOTE
- Dried watermelon is best used as a snack food.

FRUIT AND NUT TREATS

Dried watermelon is usually eaten as is — it tastes like chewy candy. Since rehydrated watermelon loses flavor and gains a mushy texture, I prefer to use it dried in trail mixes or fruit snacks.

1½ cups mixed nuts, toasted
½ cup dried watermelon
½ cup chopped dried dates
½ cup mixed dried red and green
  grapes (raisins)
¼ cup chopped dried apples
1 tsp. lemon juice
1-2 tbs. dark rum
confectioners' sugar or shredded coconut
  for coating

Mix toasted nuts and chopped fruit in a large bowl. Add lemon juice and enough rum to hold mixture together. Form into small log-shaped pieces and roll in confectioners' sugar or coconut until coated. Air dry for at least 24 hours before eating.

ZUCCHINI

PREPARATION: Wash, trim, cut into 1/4-inch slices or grate.

PRETREATMENT: Not necessary.

DEHYDRATE: Dry at 100° for about 12 hours, until brittle.

REHYDRATE: Soak in hot water for about 30 minutes; drain.

NOTE
- Dried grated zucchini is great for baked goods, such as breads or cakes.
- Dried sliced zucchini works well in casserole dishes.
- Dried sliced zucchini can be seasoned before drying and used as chips for snacking.

WHOLE WHEAT VEGETABLE PIZZA

Makes one 14-inch pizza

Here is a healthy alternative to a favorite food that is really appreciated by kids. Greek or black olives are a nice addition, or even a sprinkling of capers for the adventurous types. Other topping alternatives include spinach, red onion, bell peppers or even jalapeños.

CRUST

1 pkg. active dry yeast
1 cup warm water
1 tsp. sugar
1½ cups all-purpose flour
1 cup whole wheat flour
1 tsp. salt
1 tbs. olive oil

Dissolve yeast in warm water. Add sugar and about 1 cup of the all-purpose flour to reach the consistency of pancake batter or "sponge." Let stand for 30 minutes in a warm place, until slightly risen.

Beat sponge with a spoon and add remaining flour and salt. With a food processor, process until mixture forms a ball; add oil and process for 40 seconds. Or, add remaining ingredients to sponge and knead with a mixer's dough hook or by hand until smooth. Let dough rest for about 10 minutes. Stretch dough to fit a 14-inch pizza pan.

TOPPING

1 cup rehydrated sliced zucchini
1 cup rehydrated sliced mushrooms
½ cup rehydrated sliced onion
2 tbs. olive oil
salt and pepper to taste
3 large tomatoes, seeded and chopped
2 tbs. tomato paste

1 tsp. dried oregano
½ tsp. dried basil
½ tsp. salt
¼ tsp. pepper
12 oz. mozzarella cheese, shredded
sliced black or Greek olives to taste,
   optional

Heat oven to 450°. In a skillet, sauté zucchini, mushrooms and onion in olive oil until tender-crisp and season with salt and pepper. Mix tomatoes with tomato paste, oregano, basil, ½ tsp. salt and ¼ tsp. pepper. Spread tomato mixture on pizza crust and sprinkle with grated cheese, sautéed vegetables and olives, if using. Bake on a low oven rack for about 25 minutes, until the edges of crust are browned and cheese is bubbly.

NOTE: For a puffier crust, let shaped dough rise for about 30 minutes before adding topping.

CHOCOLATE ZUCCHINI CAKE

Zucchini grows in abundance, especially here in the Pacific Northwest. Zucchini gives a cake moisture and adds nutrients. This cake is delicious frosted with your favorite chocolate frosting or sprinkled with confectioners' sugar.

3 eggs
1½ cups sugar
1½ tsp. vanilla extract
½ cup vegetable oil
2 cups all-purpose flour
⅓ cup unsweetened cocoa powder
1 tsp. baking soda

1½ tsp. baking powder
1 tsp. cinnamon
¼ tsp. salt
¾ cup buttermilk
2 cups rehydrated shredded zucchini
1½ cups chopped toasted nuts
¾ cup dehydrated grapes (raisins)

Heat oven to 350°. Grease and flour a tube pan. With a mixer, beat eggs; add sugar and vanilla and beat well. Add oil and mix until well blended. Mix together flour, cocoa powder, baking soda, baking powder, cinnamon and salt. Add flour mixture to egg mixture along with buttermilk and mix until blended. Stir in zucchini, nuts and grapes (raisins). Pour batter into prepared pan and bake for 50 minutes, or until a knife inserted into the center comes out clean. Cool for 10 minutes and invert onto a plate. Cool.

140   FRUITS AND VEGETABLES

FRUIT AND VEGETABLE LEATHERS

If desired, sprinkle leathers before drying with chopped nuts, coconut, chopped dates, cereal, granola, raisins, sesame seeds, sunflower kernels or similar items to add texture.

PREPARATION

Fruit: Wash fresh, ripe fruit. Remove stems, peel and remove any bruised sections. Puree fruit with a blender until very smooth and easy to pour. Taste puree. If fruit needs sweetening, add 1 tbs. honey, fruit juice concentrate or white corn syrup per quart of puree at a time until desired sweetness is obtained (do not sweeten with sugar, as it tends to crystallize, causing a granular texture). If desired, add powdered spices or flavored extracts to taste for additional flavor.

Vegetables: Wash vegetables, peel if desired and steam blanch until tender. Chop vegetables into pieces and puree with a blender until very smooth and easy to pour. If needed, add a small amount of water achieve pouring consistency. Combining several varieties of vegetables usually produces a better flavor. If desired, add powdered spices or herbs to taste before drying. Certain vegetables, such as tomatoes, may have a tendency towards bitterness. To reduce this, add a little sweetener to taste.

PRETREATMENT: Not necessary.

Continued on the next page

DEHYDRATE: Spread puree about ¼-inch thick on solid plastic trays, or on heavy plastic wrap that has been stretched over regular drying trays. Leave a 1-inch border around the edges to accommodate spreading during dehydrating. Dry at 100° for about 16 to 18 hours, until pliable. Times may vary according to type of fruit or vegetable used and the thickness of the puree.

STORAGE: Remove leathers from the dehydrator and, while still warm, roll up cigar-fashion. Wrap plastic wrap around the outside of the roll and store in an airtight container. If desired, store nut-covered leathers in the refrigerator or freezer to keep the nuts from becoming rancid.

NOTE
- Canned fruit and vegetables can be used to make leathers. Drain fruit and puree with a blender. A small amount of lemon juice can freshen the flavor.
- Leathers can be wrapped around a filling for a great appetizer or dessert. Fill with cream cheese, chocolate, jam, nut butter, cheese or thick fruit filling. Cut filled leathers into 1-inch rounds.

FRUIT LEATHER VARIATIONS

Use fruit juice concentrate, honey or white corn syrup for sweeteners.

APPLE-RAISIN: 6 cups chopped apples and ½ cup chopped dried grapes (raisins).

APPLE-RHUBARB: 5 cups chopped apples, 1 cup cooked rhubarb and sweetener to taste.

APPLE-BERRY: 3 cups chopped apples, 3 cups berries and sweetener to taste.

APRICOT-PLUM: 3 cups chopped apricots, 3 cups chopped plums and sweetener to taste.

APRICOT-BANANA: 5 cups chopped apricots, 1 cup mashed bananas and vanilla extract to taste.

BANANA-PINEAPPLE: 4 cups mashed bananas, 2 cups chopped pineapple and sweetener to taste.

BANANA-PEANUT BUTTER: 4 cups mashed bananas, 2 cups crunchy peanut butter and sweetener to taste.

Continued on the next page

STRAWBERRY-RHUBARB: 4 cups chopped strawberries, 2 cups chopped cooked rhubarb and sweetener to taste.

CRANBERRY-APPLE: 3 cups cranberries, 3 cups chopped apples and sweetener to taste.

PEACH-PEAR: 3 cups chopped peaches, 3 cups chopped pears, 1 tsp. cinnamon and sweetener to taste.

CHERRY-APPLE: 4 cups cherries, 2 cups chopped apples, 1 tsp. lemon juice and sweetener to taste.

GRAPE-APPLE: 2 cups grapes and 4 cups chopped apples.

CARROT-APPLE: 4 cups cooked and mashed carrots, 2 cups chopped apple and a pinch cinnamon and/or ground ginger.

PARSNIP-SWEET POTATO: 3 cups cooked mashed parsnips, 3 cups cooked mashed carrots, 1 tbs. lemon juice, optional, and 1 tsp. grated fresh lemon peel (zest), optional.

TROUBLE-SHOOTING LEATHER PROBLEMS

- **Puree is too thin**: Combine puree with thicker purees or cook to reduce the water content (note that cooking can destroy nutrients and reduce flavor).
- **Puree is too thick**: Add fruit juice or water to the puree or combine with thinner purees.
- **Leather sticks to drying surface**: Coat or spray the tray or plastic wrap with a small amount of vegetable oil before pouring puree. Do not use foil or waxed paper. High-pectin fruits, such as berries, should be mixed with other fruits.
- **Leather dries unevenly**: Tilt and shake drying tray until puree is evenly distributed. Rotate the drying trays during dehydrating.
- **Leather is brittle**: Check the temperature of the dehydrator with an oven thermometer. If the temperature is too high, reduce the heat.
- **Leather is too dark**: Add ascorbic acid to the puree to help prevent darkening. Sometimes cooking the fruit ahead of time helps, but it can destroy nutrients and can reduce flavor. Also, air and light exposure during storage can darken leathers.
- **Leather has mold**: Make sure leather is dried sufficiently before storing and is not exposed to moisture during storage.

MEAT OR POULTRY JERKY

PREPARATION: Use lean meat or poultry, such as flank steak, top round steak, turkey breast or chicken breast, and remove any bones and visible fat, which can turn rancid over time. Cut meat or poultry against the grain into long narrow strips about $1/4$-inch thick. To make cutting easier, partially freeze the meat or poultry.

PRETREATMENT: Marinate, if desired, (see pages 148-49) for at least 1 hour and up to 24 hours in the refrigerator. Stir mixture occasionally and make sure all meat is covered. Drain before dehydrating.

DEHYDRATE: Dry meat or poultry in a single layer at 145° for about 5 to 10 hours (usually about 6 hours), or until meat is pliable, but does not break when bent. Check jerky occasionally and remove any fat from the surface of the drying meat or poultry with a paper towel. The dehydrating process will "cook" the food sufficiently to make it safe for eating.

STORAGE: Cool meat or poultry jerky thoroughly and store in airtight containers. You may wish to store jerkies in the freezer unless planning to use them immediately to guarantee safety.

NOTES

- Beef jerky is the most popular dried meat, but don't limit yourself just to beef. The same technique and most marinades work well for game meats and poultry.
- For estimating the amount of meat you will need, remember that meat will dry to about 1/4 of its fresh weight.
- Dried meats and poultry can be reconstituted by themselves, or mixed with rehydrated dried vegetables to use in hot dishes like casseroles, stews and soups.
- Dried meat can be a quick snack when participating in all kinds of outdoor sports.
- Reconstituting finely chopped or powdered dried meats with buttermilk or mayonnaise and a little water, if necessary, produces a great base for sandwich spreads. Add seasonings and chopped pickles if desired.
- Finely chopped or powdered dried meat or poultry can be rehydrated with water, chicken stock or milk to use for feeding babies or people who have trouble eating solid foods.
- Indians made *pemmican*, a powdered mixture of dried meat, fat, berries and/or dried corn and grains, for survival. Adding spices and herbs to the mixture make a more palatable meal for avid outdoors people who want to experiment.

JERKY VARIATIONS

Makes about ½ pound

There are several ways to add flavors to your jerkies before drying.

TRADITIONAL MEAT OR POULTRY JERKY

½ cup soy sauce
½ cup Worcestershire sauce
2 tbs. ketchup
1¼ tsp. salt
½ tsp. pepper

2 tbs. brown or granulated sugar
1 clove garlic, well mashed
½ tsp. onion powder
2 lb. lean meat or poultry, cut into
    ¼-inch strips

Mix all ingredients together. Follow instructions on page 146 for making jerky.

SWEET AND SOUR MEAT OR POULTRY JERKY

Makes about ¾ pound

½ cup balsamic or red wine vinegar
1 tsp. garlic powder
2 tsp. salt
¾ cup pineapple juice
½ cup brown sugar, packed

¼ cup soy sauce
¼ tsp. ground ginger
3 lb. lean meat or poultry, cut into
    ¼-inch strips

Mix all ingredients together. Follow instructions on page 146 for making jerky, marinating for at least 6 hours.

SMOKY MEAT OR POULTRY JERKY

Makes about ½ pound

2 tsp. chili powder
2 tsp. dried garlic powder
2 tsp. dried onion powder
2 tsp. ground black pepper
2 tbs. salt
1 tsp. brown sugar

½ tsp. cayenne pepper
½-1 tsp. Liquid Smoke
1 cup water
2 lb. lean meat or poultry, cut into
   ¼-inch strips

Mix all ingredients together. Follow instructions for making jerky on page 146, marinating for at least 6 hours.

SPICY MEAT OR POULTRY JERKY

Makes about ¾ pound

6 tbs. vegetable oil
1 cup soy sauce
6 tbs. brown sugar, packed
3 tbs. sherry
2 tsp. finely minced garlic

¼ tsp. ground ginger
few dashes Tabasco Sauce, optional
3 lb. lean meat or poultry, cut into
   ¼-inch strips

Mix all ingredients together. Follow instructions for making jerky on page 146.

NOTE: Bottled marinades, teriyaki sauces, barbecue sauces and even dressings are a good alternative to these marinades if time is limited.

GROUND MEAT OR POULTRY JERKY

PREPARATION: Use lean or extra-lean ground meats or poultry and mix with spices, sauces or flavorings. Some commercial dehydrator companies also sell jerky spice mixes. If you have a jerky press, follow the manufacturer's instructions. Or, roll out the meat with a rolling pin between 2 pieces of waxed paper until about 1/8-inch thick. Remove top layer of waxed paper, invert bottom layer onto tray, peel off paper and discard.

PRETREATMENT: Not necessary.

DEHYDRATE: Place rolled meat or poultry on solid plastic trays that have been covered with plastic wrap. Dry at 145° for about 1 to 2 hours, or until meat can be handled without falling apart. Remove meat from trays and plastic wrap. With a paper towel, blot off any fat on the surface of the meat. With scissors, cut meat into 1-x-6-inch strips and transfer strips to regular drying trays. Continue drying until meat is pliable, about 1 hour. Check periodically for fat on the meat surface and blot with paper towels.

STORAGE: Store in airtight containers in the freezer.

SPICED GROUND MEAT OR POULTRY JERKY

Makes about ¾ pound

3 lb. lean ground meat or poultry
2 tbs. Worcestershire sauce
1 tsp. dried onion powder
1 tsp. brown sugar
¼ tsp. pepper
1 tbs. tomato paste

Mix all ingredients together. In a skillet, sauté a small amount of mixture until cooked through. Taste and adjust seasonings. Follow instructions for making ground meat or poultry jerky on page 150.

ITALIAN GROUND MEAT OR POULTRY JERKY

Makes about 1 pound

4 lb. lean ground meat or poultry
3 cups grated Parmesan cheese
1 tsp. dried oregano
2 tsp. dried parsley
2 tsp. seasoned salt
½ tsp. dried basil
2 tsp. dried garlic powder

Mix all ingredients together. In a skillet, sauté a small amount of mixture until cooked through. Taste and adjust seasonings. Follow instructions for making ground meat or poultry jerky on page 150.

DRIED COOKED MEAT OR POULTRY

PREPARATION: Cook meat and trim any excess fat. Cut into ½-inch cubes.

PRETREATMENT: Not necessary.

DEHYDRATE: Dry at 145° for about 6 to 12 hours, or until meat appears hard and crisp with no signs of moisture. If desired, reduce the temperature to about 125° towards the end of the drying time for more tender results.

STORAGE: Store in an airtight container and freeze.

REHYDRATE: Soak dried cooked meats in boiling water or broth for about 45 minutes to 1 hour. Simmer over low heat for 20 minutes.

FISH JERKY

Fish must be soaked in salt brine (1 cup salt to 2 cups cold water) before drying.

PREPARATION: Use only very fresh and lean fish fillets. Fishes high in oil, such as salmon or smelt, do not dry as well. Cut fish fillets into $1/4$-inch strips.

PRETREATMENT: Soak fish in salt brine solution for 30 minutes. Remove and rinse with cold water; drain. Coat fish with desired cure mixture and place in an airtight container. Refrigerate for about 6 hours.

DEHYDRATE: Place cured fish on drying trays in a single layer. Dry at 145° for about 12 to 14 hours, or until pliable, but not crumbly.

STORAGE: Cool completely and store in airtight containers in the freezer.

FISH JERKY VARIATIONS

Don't let the high amount of salt in these recipes scare you. It is necessary to properly preserve the fish or "cure" it and to achieve the proper texture when dried.

TRADITIONAL FISH JERKY
Makes about 2 lb.

2 tbs. salt
2 tsp. dried onion powder
1 tsp. dried garlic powder
1 tbs. Liquid Smoke, or to taste

$\frac{1}{4}$ cup soy sauce
dash Tabasco Sauce
4 lb. lean fish fillets, cut into $\frac{1}{4}$-inch strips

Mix salt with onion and garlic powder. Mix liquid ingredients together and spread over fish; sprinkle with salt mixture. Follow instructions for making fish jerky on page 153.

HERB-FLAVORED FISH JERKY
Makes about 2 lb.

2 tbs. salt
1 tsp. dried celery flakes
$\frac{1}{4}$ cup dried parsley flakes
$\frac{1}{2}$ tsp. crushed dried bay leaf
1 tsp. pepper

$\frac{1}{4}$ tsp. dried thyme
2 tsp. onion powder
$\frac{1}{4}$ cup dry white wine
4 lb. lean fish fillets, cut into $\frac{1}{4}$-inch strips

Mix salt with other dry ingredients. Rub fish strips with white wine and sprinkle with salt mixture. Follow instructions for making fish jerky on page 153.

DEHYDRATED PREPARED FOOD

Yield: varies

You can successfully dry many different kinds of canned or homemade prepared foods, such as tomato sauce, pasta sauce, stew, baked beans, chili and even thick soup. They make quick, lightweight "hikers'" food.

PREPARATION: Cool prepared food slightly if hot.

PRETREATMENT: Not necessary.

DEHYDRATE: Pour prepared food onto solid plastic trays or standard trays covered with plastic wrap. Dry at 145° for about 10 hours, until brittle. Sauces can be dried like fruit leathers: when pliable, roll and store using the same technique (see page 142).

STORAGE: Cool completely and store in airtight jars in the freezer.

REHYDRATE: Stir dried food with a small amount of boiling water at a time, checking every 10 minutes to see if it needs additional hot water. This will prevent the flavor from becoming too diluted. Once you know about how much water the dried food can take, you can reproduce the same results next time.

BABY FOOD

Dehydrated fruits and vegetables make wonderful, wholesome baby food. The first step is to make vegetable or fruit powder: using vegetables or fruits that are very dry and brittle, chop into small pieces and whirl in a blender until powdery. Store fruit and vegetable powders in airtight glass jars in a dark, cool area until ready to use.

VEGETABLE BABY FOOD

Makes 1 cup

1 cup hot water, milk or goat's milk   ⅓ cup powdered dried vegetables

Pour hot water or milk over vegetable powder and let stand for about 20 minutes. Pour mixture into a blender container and blend until smooth.

MEAT AND VEGETABLE BABY FOOD

Makes 1½ cups

1 cup hot water or milk   3 tbs. chopped cooked meat
⅓ cup powdered dried vegetables

Pour hot water or milk over vegetable powder and let stand for about 20 minutes. Pour mixture into a blender container, add chopped cooked meat and blend until smooth.

FRUIT BABY FOOD

Makes 1 cup

½ cup dried fruit or chopped fruit
  leather

½-1 cup hot water

Chop dried fruit into small pieces. Pour hot water over fruit to cover and let stand for about 30 minutes. Pour mixture into a blender container and blend until smooth, adding more hot water if puree is too thick. Strain if desired.

VARIATION: FRUIT AND CEREAL BABY FOOD
Add fruit puree to 1 cup prepared baby cereal. Makes 2 cups.

FRUIT PUDDING

Makes 2 cups

1 cup boiling water
½ cup chopped dried fruit
2 egg yolks
¾ cup milk

1 tbs. cornstarch
honey, fruit juice concentrate or sugar
  to taste

Pour boiling water over dried fruit and let stand for about 20 minutes. Pour mixture into a blender container and blend until smooth. Add egg yolks and milk and blend until smooth. Add cornstarch and honey and blend. Transfer to a small saucepan and cook over medium heat until thickened. Remove from heat, cool and chill.

DRIED HERBS

The leaves of herbs should be green and tender, harvested just before the plant begins to flower. Always dry herbs at a low temperature, as high temperatures can destroy herbs' natural oils.

PREPARATION: Rinse herbs with cold water and shake off excess. Pat dry with paper towels and remove any dead, mushy or discolored leaves.

PRETREATMENT: Not necessary.

DEHYDRATE: Spread herbs loosely on a tray and dry at 95° to 100° for about 3 to 5 hours, until brittle. Herbs with larger leaves will take longer.

STORAGE: Store dried herbs in tightly closed containers in a cool, dark place. Do not store in paper bags, which will absorb the natural oils and reduce the potency of the herb.

NOTE

- It is best to dry herbs separately from other foods. Drying with produce creates a more moist environment and will increase herbs' drying time.

- Herbs can be dried while they are still on the stem. When completely dry and brittle, strip leaves from stems.
- Do not grind the leaves into a powder before storing. Just before using, grind dried herbs into a powder with a mortar and pestle, or crush them in your hand.
- Most dried herbs have 3 to 4 times the potency of fresh herbs.
- 8 oz. fresh herbs will yield about 1 oz. dried.
- Dried herbs should keep well for 6 months to 1 year.

HERBAL TEAS

Steep the following in hot water until desired strength is reached.

- Chamomile, hops and valerian.
- Dried spearmint, chamomile and blueberry leaves.
- Dried orange peel and blackberry leaves.
- Rose hips, dried orange peel and ginger.
- Dried spearmint leaves, peppermint leaves and dried lemon peel.

YOGURT

Makes 1 quart

An exact temperature is crucial when making yogurt. Temperatures too high will curdle the yogurt. Temperatures too low will take the yogurt considerably longer to thicken. You can use any type of milk to suit your personal preference. To make yogurt, you will need special containers that are sold as an accessory to the dehydrator.

1 qt. milk
½ cup instant powdered milk
2-3 tbs. purchased plain yogurt, or
   1 tbs. yogurt starter

flavored extracts to taste, optional
chopped dried fruits to taste, optional
honey, fruit juice concentrate or corn
   syrup to taste, optional

In a saucepan, mix milk and powdered milk. Heat until steaming, remove from heat and cool to 110°. If using purchased yogurt, mix well with cooled milk. If using yogurt starter, add yogurt starter to ⅓ cup of the milk and mix well. Return mixture to remaining milk and mix well. Place a thermometer in the dehydrator and adjust the controls until the temperature reaches 108°. Pour yogurt-making containers and cover. Place containers in dehydrator and dry at 108° for 2 to 4 hours, or longer if temperature is too low. Remove from dehydrator and cool. If desired, stir in flavored extracts, dried fruits and/or sweeteners to taste.

YOGURT SNACK DROPS

These make an excellent, healthy snack for kids.

flavored yogurt
chopped toasted nuts or dried fruit, optional

Drop yogurt by half-teaspoonfuls on oiled solid sheets or regular sheets covered with plastic wrap. If desired, sprinkle yogurt drops with chopped toasted nuts or dried fruit. Dry at 135° for about 10 hours, until chewy. Remove drops from sheet while warm. Chill and store in a covered jar or contatiner in the refrigerator or freezer.

YOGURT ROLLS

Send a yogurt roll-up as a lunch box treat. Or, roll it together with fruit leather, cut it into 1-inch pieces and serve.

about 5 cups flavored yogurt
chopped toasted nuts, coconut or dried fruit, optional

Spread yogurt on an oiled solid sheet or regular sheet covered with plastic wrap until about 1/8-inch thick. If desired, sprinkle with chopped nuts, coconut or dried fruit. Dry at 125° for about 10 hours, until leathery. Remove from sheet while warm and roll. Store covered in the refrigerator or freezer.

DRIED NUTS

PREPARATION: Shell fresh nuts, if desired. Rinse nuts with hot water, which removes dust as well as a residual oil.

PRETREATMENT: Not necessary.

DEHYDRATE: Spread nuts on trays in a single layer. Dry unshelled nuts at 90° to 100° for about 24 to 48 hours, until brittle. Dry shelled nuts for about about 10 hours. To test, open a shelled nut and taste: the nutmeat should be tender, but not shriveled; cool.

STORAGE: Store cooled nuts in glass jars or airtight plastic bags below 70°. For longer storage, freeze nuts to prevent the oils from becoming rancid. When ready to use frozen nuts, bring jar to room temperature before proceeding. The frozen nuts will immediately draw moisture from the environment, which leads to possible mold or faster rancidity.

NUT AND FRUIT MIX

This is only one combination of fruit and nuts. You can create endless possible mixtures of this high-protein energy food.

1 lb. dried shelled almonds, toasted
1 lb. dried shelled Brazil nuts, toasted
1 lb. dried shelled cashew nuts, toasted
½ lb. pine nuts, toasted
½ lb. mixed dried red and green grapes (raisins)
¼ cup Marsala wine, sweet vermouth or fruit juice
¼ cup shredded dried coconut
¼ cup salted sunflower kernels
¼ cup chopped dried fruit, such as apricots, pears or apples
salt to taste, optional
Worcestershire sauce to taste, optional

Mix nuts together and set aside. In a saucepan, mix dried grapes (raisins) and wine and bring to a boil. Immediately reduce heat to low and simmer until liquid has evaporated, about 20 minutes. Remove from heat and cool. Combine raisin mixture with remaining ingredients, including nuts, and mix well. If desired, add salt and/or Worcestershire sauce to taste.

CROUTONS

Croutons are very easy to make and a great way to use bread before it molds.

PREPARATION: Cut leftover bread into $\frac{1}{2}$-inch squares, with or without the crusts. Crusts are usually removed when bread will become crumbs to use for coating and frying. Use dried crusts as toppings for casseroles.

PRETREATMENT: Not necessary.

DEHYDRATE: Dry bread cubes at 145° for about 2 to 3 hours, until crisp.

STORAGE: Store in an airtight glass or plastic container in a cool, dark place for up to 3 months.

NOTE

- For seasoned croutons, mix together 1 tsp. salt, 1 tsp. paprika and 3 tbs. finely grated Parmesan cheese or minced fresh herbs and place in a paper bag. Toss dried croutons with a little melted butter in a skillet. While hot, drop croutons into paper bag and shake to coat with seasonings.

- For breadcrumbs, process dried croutons into fine crumbs with a blender or food processor.

DRIED FLOWERS

Many flowers can be dried in the dehydrator, but be prepared to experiment a little and keep the temperature very low, which retains the natural oils. The best condition for drying flowers is a clean, dry, warm, dark and well-ventilated area, which makes a dehydrator an ideal setting. Flowers will retain the best color and condition when dried quickly.

PREPARATION: Use dry flowers, which are best if picked after the dew has dried and before the damp night air sets in. Dehydrate the flowers as soon as possible after picking. Strip off the leaves, or if you prefer to keep the foliage, discard brown or damaged leaves.

PRETREATMENT: Not necessary.

DEHYDRATE: Place flowers on the drying trays in a single layer, avoiding overlapping. The drying time will vary considerably, depending on the size of the flower and the amount of foliage. Dry at 100° for 6 to 72 hours, until petals are stiff.

STORAGE: To avoid crushing the brittle flower petals, store dried flowers in a covered box in a dry place.

POTPOURRI

Display your colorful potpourri in beautiful glass dishes. If the potpourri begins to lose some of its potency, add a few more drops of essential oil. Essential oils can be found in craft stores, new-age supply stores and some health food stores.

HERB AND FLOWER POTPOURRI
Makes about 11 cups

6 cups rose petals
1 cup dried thyme
1 cup dried rosemary
1 cup dried sweet marjoram
1 cup dried lavender
1 cup dried sweet basil

6 bay leaves, crushed
1 tbs. allspice berries
2 tbs. dried lemon peel
2 tbs. dried orange peel
1 tsp. anise seeds

Mix all ingredients and store in an airtight jar in a cool, dark area until ready to use.

MINT POTPOURRI
Makes about 4 cups

2 cups dried lavender
1 cup dried whole mint leaves
½ cup dried thyme
¼ cup dried rosemary
few drops essential oil

few dried geranium petals
few dried blue bachelor's buttons
few dried flower petals, such as
    delphinium or rose

Mix all ingredients and store in an airtight container until ready to use.

INDEX

Serve creative, easy, nutritious meals with nitty gritty® cookbooks

Wraps and Roll-Ups
Easy Vegetarian Cooking
Party Fare: Irresistible Nibbles
    for Every Occasion
Cappuccino/Espresso: The Book of
    Beverages
Fresh Vegetables
Cooking with Fresh Herbs
Cooking with Chile Peppers
The Dehydrator Cookbook
Recipes for the Pressure Cooker
Beer and Good Food
Unbeatable Chicken Recipes
Gourmet Gifts
From Freezer, 'Fridge and Pantry
Edible Pockets for Every Meal
Oven and Rotisserie Roasting
Risottos, Paellas and Other Rice
    Specialties
Muffins, Nut Breads and More
Healthy Snacks for Kids
100 Dynamite Desserts
Recipes for Yogurt Cheese
Sautés
Cooking in Porcelain

Casseroles
The Toaster Oven Cookbook
Skewer Cooking on the Grill
Creative Mexican Cooking
Marinades
No Salt, No Sugar, No Fat Cookbook
Quick and Easy Pasta Recipes
Cooking in Clay
Deep Fried Indulgences
The Garlic Cookbook
From Your Ice Cream Maker
The Best Pizza is Made at Home
The Best Bagels are Made at Home
Convection Oven Cookery
The Steamer Cookbook
The Pasta Machine Cookbook
The Versatile Rice Cooker
The Bread Machine Cookbook
The Bread Machine Cookbook II
The Bread Machine Cookbook III
The Bread Machine Cookbook IV:
    Whole Grains & Natural Sugars
The Bread Machine Cookbook V:
    Favorite Recipes from 100
    Kitchens

The Bread Machine Cookbook VI:
    Hand-Shaped Breads from the
    Dough Cycle
Worldwide Sourdoughs from Your
    Bread Machine
Entrées from Your Bread Machine
The New Blender Book
The Sandwich Maker Cookbook
Waffles
The Coffee Book
The Juicer Book I and II
Bread Baking
The 9 x 13 Pan Cookbook
Recipes for the Loaf Pan
Low Fat American Favorites
Healthy Cooking on the Run
Favorite Seafood Recipes
New International Fondue Cookbook
Favorite Cookie Recipes
Cooking for 1 or 2
The Well Dressed Potato
Extra-Special Crockery Pot Recipes
Slow Cooking
The Wok

For a free catalog, write or call: Bristol Publishing Enterprises, Inc.
P.O. Box 1737, San Leandro, CA 94577 (800) 346-4889

Visit our website at
www.bristolcookbooks.com